W0017017

GLOBAL AGGRESSION

The Case for World Standards and Bold US Action Challenging Philip Morris and RJR Nabisco

An INFACT Report

The photos on the cover are part of INFACT's Human Toll of Tobacco Project—a collection of photos and stories of people who are suffering or have died from tobacco-related illnesses.

The Human Toll of Tobacco Project began in response to Congressional testimony by a former RJR Nabisco executive that the people who die each year from tobacco are just "computer-generated numbers."

Photos have come in from all over the US and many regions of the world, and are part of a 200-foot-long banner. The banner made a memorable debut at the Philip Morris and RJR Nabisco Annual Meetings in the Spring of 1995. The display is now being used in public events from New Mexico to Beijing, China, from New York to Santiago, Chile, calling on tobacco industry leaders and their political allies to account for their role in this preventable epidemic.

Additional photos for the Human Toll of Tobacco Project may be sent directly to INFACT.

Cover photos used with permission.

GLOBAL AGGRESSION

The Case for World Standards and Bold US Action Challenging Philip Morris and RJR Nabisco

INFACT's 1998 People's Annual Report

The Apex Press
New York

© 1998 by INFACT

Published by The Apex Press, an imprint of the Council on International and Public Affairs,
    777 United Nations Plaza, Suite 3C,
    New York, NY 10017
    Telephone/fax: 800/316-APEX (2739)
    E-mail: cipany@igc.apc.org

Published in cooperation with:
    INFACT
    256 Hanover Street
    Boston, MA 02113
    Telephone: 617/742-4583
    Fax: 617/367-0191
    E-mail: infact@igc.apc.org

Library of Congress Cataloging-in-Publication Data has been applied for.

ISBN 0-945257-95-3

Cover design by S. Warren Hurley
Typesetting and layout by Peggy Hurley
Printed in the United States of America

® GCIU 745-C

TABLE OF CONTENTS

INFACT dedicates this Exposé to the millions of people around the world who have needlessly lost loved ones to Big Tobacco's deadly legacy.
Hope is in the hearts of those who continue to mobilize for the health and welfare of coming generations.

ACKNOWLEDGMENTS

Popular opposition to the deadly tobacco industry derives its force from the spirit of social change movements, exemplifying the essence of genuine democracy. With relentless attention to the tobacco corporations bent on peddling their hazardous products, activists from around the world are coming closer to securing concrete tobacco control measures. INFACT honors all of you who are committed to securing these changes.

INFACT thanks its activists, donors, members, and organizational allies, families and friends who have helped make this Exposé possible.

Special thanks and our deep appreciation go to our international allies who wrote sections of this Report: Mary Assunta, Consumers Association of Penang, Malaysia; and Konstantin Krasovsky, Alcohol and Drug Information Center, Ukraine.

Our thanks to tobacco control advocates around the world who have also contributed to the Report: Dr. Varabhorn Bhumiswasdi, Ministry of Public Health, Thailand; John Bloom, Manager of International Issues, National Center for Tobacco Free Kids; Dr. José Ramón Calvo Fernández, MD, Ph.D., University of Las Palmas de Gran Canaria, Spain; Dr. Greg Connolly, Massachusetts Department of Public Health; Rob Cunningham, Senior Policy Analyst, Canadian Cancer Society; Dr. Luiza Costa e Silva Goldfarb, National Institute of Cancer, Brazil; Dr. Vera Luiza da Costa e Silva, National Coordination for Tobacco Control and Cancer Primary Prevention–Contapp, Brazil; Debra Efroymson, PATH Canada; Mervi Hara, Director, Finland ASH; Grover Ho, Hong Kong; Ruben Israel, Head, GLOBALink Information Services, International Union Against Cancer (UICC); Dr. George Katarov, National Center for Health Promotion, Bulgaria; Eva Kralikova, MD, Ph.D., First

Faculty of Medicine, Charles University, Czech Republic; Karen Lewis, Deputy Director of Tobacco Control Projects, and her colleagues at the Advocacy Institute; Judith Mackay, Director, Asian Consultancy on Tobacco Control; Jane Martin, Information and Policy Manager, Victorian Smoking and Health Program, Australia; Nobuko Nakano, Women's Action on Smoking, Japan; Paul Nordgren, Tobacco Control Programme, Swedish National Institute of Public Health; Bung On Ritthiphakdee, Director, ASH Thailand; Viktorija Rehar, Institute of Public Health, Slovenia; Ken Sheppard, Tobacco Action Committee, South Africa; Tomas Stanikas, Kaunas Medical Academy, Lithuania; Scott Thompson, Health Promotion Foundation and Center for Cancer Epidemiology and Prevention, Poland; Anna White, Fulbright Fellow 1997-98, Senegal; Derek Yach, World Health Organization; Chng Chee Yeong, Ministry of Health, Singapore; and Dr. Zarihah Mohd Zain, Disease Control Division, Ministry of Health, Malaysia.

To Wendy Fassett and Eric Rosenberg whose help on this project covered many areas; and to Christine Andersen, Zell Draz, Daniel R. and Jan Lewis, Robin Lloyd, Christopher Lloyd, Henry Lord, and Harold and Louise Nielsen, whose leadership makes all of this campaigning possible: thank you.

As always, INFACT's Board of Directors (Greg Akili, Wayne Baker, Kim Buzan, Joby Gelbspan, Dick Harding, Michael Ho, Kelle Louaillier, Jerome Scott, Makani Themba, Lucinda Wykle-Rosenberg) has provided essential guidance and support. We would also like to recognize INFACT's excellent crew of interns: Ed Brolin, Alpana Kumar, and Nick Yoder; and the dedicated staff of INFACT: Sue Andersen, Todd Basch, Melissa Breach, Jaime Becker, Karla Capers, Kim Foltz, John Hocevar, Beth Hurst, Kelle Louaillier, Sangita Nayak, Rebecca Pearl, Claribel Ramos, Dave Schneider, Sandra Scott, Amanda Toering, and Lucinda Wykle-Rosenberg.

Many thanks also to Cynthia T. Morehouse and Peggy Hurley of The Apex Press for producing this book in record time.

We would also like to acknowledge the thousands of INFACT members who have supported us throughout the years. You have provided a solid foundation for INFACT's work to grow on. Together, we will forge ahead on the road of progressive social change.

Kathryn Mulvey
Boston, March 1998

INTRODUCTION

Will the Real Philip Morris Please Stand Up?

> It is our intention to defend our industry and the rights of our consumers as briskly as we possibly can, as strenuously as we possibly can. — *Philip Morris CEO Geoffrey Bible, quoted in the* New York Times, *June 22, 1994*
>
> We believe that we are absolutely right in all of the positions we take on these issues. And we are fighting very hard for what we believe in. — *Philip Morris CEO Geoffrey Bible, letter to shareholders, February 1995*
>
> Our one all-consuming ambition is to create wealth for the owners of Philip Morris. — *Philip Morris CEO Geoffrey Bible, letter to shareholders, February 1995*

> Real solutions include a "willingness to make fundamental changes in our way of doing business." — *Philip Morris CEO Geoffrey Bible, in testimony before the House Commerce Committee, January 1998*
>
> I don't think I'd set money above public health. I place them all at the highest ranking. — *Philip Morris CEO Geoffrey Bible, testifying in the trial of the State of Minnesota versus the tobacco industry, March 1998*

For decades, the tobacco industry has made false promises to fend off regulations, while denying and covering up the real targets of its massive marketing and promotional campaigns. In the meantime, the global tobacco epidemic has reached new proportions.

1

More than 400,000 families a year in the US lose a loved one to a tobacco-related illness. And if current trends continue, half a billion of the 5.5 billion people alive today will be wiped out by tobacco. The scope is barely conceivable.

These people are not, in the infamous words of former R.J. Reynolds CEO James Johnston, "computer-generated numbers" (testimony before U.S. House Subcommittee on Health and the Environment, April 1994). They are mothers, fathers, sisters, brothers, aunts, uncles, and dear friends:

> I am angry that my parents died so young. I am angry that they never had the chance to make it to—much less enjoy—the retirement years they earned after many years of hard work. I am especially angry to know that the tobacco industry manipulated nicotine levels in cigarettes to keep people addicted. I am angry that the industry made smoking appear so sophisticated. I am angry that my parents tried so hard so many times to quit smoking but never could. I hope INFACT's Campaign helps others to quit, prevents still others from starting, and leads Congress to find the courage to stand up to the death peddlers. — *Human Toll of Tobacco Project contributor Mary, from Florida*

There is no time to lose. We do not have the luxury to trust claims of tobacco CEOs that they are turning over a new leaf. We've heard these promises before. The last great opportunity to achieve lasting changes in US public health policy on tobacco was in the mid-1960s. We didn't succeed then—but we now have another chance to take action for corporate accountability in the US and worldwide.

Faced with this historic opportunity, we must protect the health and lives of future generations—and reclaim our democracy by asserting people's control over giant corporations that have manipulated public policy for private gain, at great cost to public health and well-being.

Why Now?

The contagion of the global tobacco epidemic is well known: an industry with vast resources to promote its deadly and addictive product, introducing aggressive promotional tactics into areas once free of tobacco advertising. Around the world, US-based tobacco transnationals Philip Morris and RJR Nabisco associate cigarettes with freedom, health, wealth, glamour, and sophistication. Here at home, they are setting out to accelerate their international expansion by marketing a raw deal to politicians and the public as aggressively as they hawk cigarettes.

> The tobacco industry is spending millions lobbying to buy themselves a deal. . . . I am here today to speak for millions of victims of the tobacco industry, and to oppose a settlement that would bar people like me from holding the tobacco industry accountable. Most of what you will hear from me today is because of my new pattern of thinking after a team of doctors cut my throat. Only after my throat was cut was I able to beat my addiction.— *INFACT activist Harold Taylor, throat-cancer survivor, in testimony before the House Judiciary Committee, February 5, 1998.*

Philip Morris and RJR Nabisco led the tobacco industry in spending $30 million to lobby the US Congress in 1997. They are pursuing a lawsuit against the FDA over regulations designed to protect children from tobacco marketing and promotion. They began 1998 with a $20 million public relations campaign designed to generate support for the proposed "global settlement." And they have taken a key role in advancing the Multilateral Agreement on Investments—essentially a global "Bill of Rights" for transnational corporations.

The lives of millions of people in the US and our worldwide neighbors are at more risk than ever before. A comprehensive survey of the tobacco transnationals' global expansion is essential to a diagnosis of how the crisis of nicotine addiction is spreading—and a prescription for how people can stop it.

Global Aggression

INFACT's 1998 People's Annual Report, *Global Aggression: The Case for World Standards and Bold US Action Challenging Philip Morris and RJR Nabisco,* exposes the worldwide practices of the two largest US-based tobacco transnationals. Using dozens of graphic examples from around the world, a wealth of data, and first-hand, personal accounts, this exposé makes Big Tobacco's abuse of power, and outrageous double standards surrounding the global tobacco epidemic, tangible:

• *Person of the Year*—Philip Morris's contest in Ukraine uses newspapers and television as "information sponsors" to slide by laws forbidding tobacco advertisements in those mediums.

The tobacco giant also expands its brand recognition with "Marlboro Adventure Team" sports promotions.

- *Salem High Country Tours*—RJR Nabisco advertised its travel agency daily on Malaysian television, broadcasting the tobacco corporation's product logo far and wide, enticing viewers with vacations. But there were no Salem tours, only Salem smoke. RJR Nabisco funded the fake travel business as a way around Malaysian restrictions on tobacco advertisements.

Malaysia and Ukraine are but two of the "expansion markets" targeted by US-based tobacco transnationals worldwide—180 for Philip Morris and 170 for RJR Nabisco.

A Time for Action

The momentum for tobacco control has been building throughout the 1990's:

The secret is out. Under intense public scrutiny and courtroom pressure, internal tobacco industry documents are coming to light, revealing a deliberate strategy of targeting teenagers:

> Today's teenager is tomorrow's potential regular customer.—*internal Philip Morris document, dated 1981, released 1/29/98*

> The [Camel] brand must increase its share penetration among the 14-24 age group, which have a new set of more liberal values and which represent tomorrow's cigarette business.—*internal RJR Nabisco document, dated 1975, released 1/14/98*

The evidence is in: RJR Nabisco developed Joe Camel in response to the phenomenal success of the Marlboro Man, described by the Philip Morris ad executive who helped design it as, "commercials that would turn rookie smokers on to Marlboro. . . . the right image to capture the youth market's fancy. . . . a perfect symbol of independence and individualistic rebellion."

The political climate is shifting. About 85 percent of US adults surveyed in August 1996 supported Food and Drug Administration (FDA) action to limit youth-oriented tobacco promotion. Even $30 million in tobacco industry lobbying expenditures in 1997 could not drown out this public consensus. Case in point: Representative

Tom Bliley of Virginia has been forced to question his longtime allies, letting them know at the outset of 1998 Commerce Committee hearings that "Four years ago I was willing to give you the benefit of the doubt. Today the burden is on you."

The stakes are mounting. With this shift in the public climate, the liabilities associated with tobacco are escalating. By proposing a "global settlement" of state lawsuits to recover tobacco-related health care costs, the industry is trying to stem the tide. But the proposed tax-deductible payout of $368.5 billion over 25 years will cover less than eight years of US health care costs to treat tobacco-related illnesses at the current rate of $50 billion annually.

Recovering Democracy

As INFACT activist Joby Gelbspan told Philip Morris shareholders at the corporation's Annual Meeting: "I came here today because I started smoking Marlboro Lights when I was fourteen, and I don't want to become part of the "Human Toll of Tobacco" Banner outside. . . . I believe my life and the lives and health of other teenagers should be more important to our government than the millions of dollars this deadly industry spends to manipulate public opinion and policy."

Outside the Philip Morris Annual Meeting in Richmond, Virginia, INFACT activists display the "Human Toll of Tobacco" Banner, protesting Philip Morris's role in tobacco marketing to young people around the world.

The tobacco industry poses a severe threat to democratic principles and practices—all the more so because these corporations have invested billions of dollars to associate their product with "freedom" and "choice." Big Tobacco:

- Champions free-market, anti-big-government rhetoric while rubbing elbows with government officials;
- Interferes in the development of national, state, and local public health policies in countries around the world;
- Drives international trade policies designed to expand corporate "rights," and to subvert democratically enacted legislation;
- Advances voluntary restrictions in the place of independently enforced laws—limits that are often not simply weaker, but insidious extensions of their marketing strategy;
- Violates the spirit of the law in many countries; and
- Breaks the law in others.

In the final hours of the millennium, transnational corporations are replacing nation-states as the dominant institutions of economic and political power. If we are to put mechanisms in place to ensure social and economic justice and protect public health, people must organize across national borders.

Since 1993, INFACT has been organizing to hold the tobacco transnationals accountable for their abuses. Through our Tobacco Industry Campaign, we've come into contact with thousands of people in the US and around the world—and been touched by their stories.

Together we call for permanent and dramatic changes in corporate and public policy to prevent tobacco promotion that appeals to children and youth. Ordinary people—whose stories are told in *Global Aggression*—are mobilizing for these changes through a combination of economic and political pressure.

You Can Make a Difference: Join the Tobacco Industry Boycott

INFACT's focus on the transnational tobacco corporations, combined with intensive grassroots organizing, are two critical components of a collective vision for a comprehensive public health agenda, including global tobacco control standards. Tobacco transnationals must change to make long-term improvements in public health possible.

The tobacco transnationals can and must be held accountable to the people whose lives they are endangering—that is, all of us. The goals of INFACT's Tobacco Industry Campaign—to stop the tobacco industry from addicting new young customers around the world, and to stop the tobacco industry from meddling in public health policy—are ambitious ones. But by focusing massive grassroots pressure on the tobacco industry's US-based, global leaders, we can take a very concrete step toward achieving those goals.

Because the root of the problem is economic—that is, fueled by the transnational corporate profit motive—consumers have a very powerful tool for change. While most of us cannot vote with Philip Morris or RJR Nabisco's board members on the future course of these corporations, we can "vote with our pocketbooks" by choosing to withhold our business from Kraft, Post, Maxwell House, and Nabisco food brands until they stop endangering our lives.

Now is our chance to build broad-based economic pressure to alter the cost-benefit ratio for Big Tobacco's deadly tobacco marketing to young people around the world, and their interference in public policymaking. Let's send our message loudly and clearly that we will not support an industry responsible for millions of deaths around the world each year.

Boycott Kraft, Post, Maxwell House, and Nabisco!

So what can *you* do? Join the Boycott, and start by spreading the word. Encourage your friends to join the Boycott. Share this book. Look around you to see how Big Tobacco impacts your community—consumer outlets, manufacturing plants, lobbying offices—and where you can find the best opportunities to have the greatest influence on Philip Morris and RJR Nabisco. Have a block party to sign your neighbors onto the Boycott, and then become a local INFACT Volunteer Organizer. Visit your local retailers to talk about stocking alternative brands. Expand to other neighborhoods, faith communities, schools, stores, local political channels. The opportunities to directly influence Big Tobacco are unlimited!

Perhaps you know Philip Morris or RJR Nabisco shareholders who would like to help stop tobacco marketing to youth around the world. Or employees with similar concerns. Some activists have even gotten state-wide public schools to participate in the Boycott.

Those are only a few ideas. You will probably come up with many other ways to help build the Boycott, once you start talking to people and looking around. And however you decide to get involved, whether you have questions, comments, or new ideas, whether you need materials or just inspiration, please contact INFACT's Campaign Headquarters. We want to hear from you.

Just remember that you *can* make a difference. When you join INFACT's Tobacco Industry Campaign and Boycott, you have the power of hundreds of thousands of concerned people working with you. Your participation *will* make a difference. Make your voice heard. Let Philip Morris and RJR Nabisco know that you will not stand for their continued subversion of the democratic process. Let them know that we value people's lives and healthy communities over profits. And let your friends and neighbors know that they, too, must speak out. Join us!

Kathryn Mulvey
INFACT Executive Director
March 1998

WORLD HEALTH IMPLICATIONS
OF INTERNATIONAL
TOBACCO EXPANSION

Tobacco-related illnesses will be the world's leading cause of death by the 2020s, and 70 percent of those deaths will occur in economically poor countries. Already, tobacco kills at least 3.5 million people per year, a figure that will rise to ten million per year by 2030 unless current trends are reversed.[1] This health crisis is spread internationally by a handful of giant corporations, with US-based Philip Morris and RJR Nabisco at the helm.

Philip Morris is the world's largest and most profitable transnational tobacco corporation and the second-largest food corporation, with $55 billion in annual revenues.[2] Philip Morris owns Marlboro, the world's top-selling cigarette brand,[3] and the #1 overall consumer brand.[4] If Marlboro were separated from Philip Morris, the brand would rank about #100 on the Fortune 500 list.[5] Philip Morris also owns Kraft Foods, with well-known brands such as Post, Maxwell House, and Jacobs Suchard.

RJR Nabisco is a $17-billion tobacco and food conglomerate, and the world's third largest tobacco corporation, following Philip Morris and British American Tobacco (B.A.T).[6] RJR Nabisco owns the fourth- and fifth-ranked cigarette brands worldwide, Winston and Camel.[7] The tobacco and food giant derives 54 percent of its profits from international sources,[8] with over half of its 1996 revenues stemming from its Nabisco food division. Outside the US, Latin America is its key market for food products.[9]

Even as international health experts are struggling to make progress on infectious diseases, tobacco is eliminating that progress. It is a preventable epidemic that imposes an impossible burden on many regions of the world. According to the World Health Organization, adolescent smoking has increased all over the world since 1990. Most international health experts agree that a key factor in the rise is the growing popularity of US cigarette brands fueled by youth-oriented marketing by the US tobacco corporations, particularly in areas previously unexposed to the slick advertising of the tobacco transnationals.[10] **Philip Morris has increased its sales of cigarettes abroad by almost 80 percent since 1990.**[11] The tobacco transnationals make up 40 percent of global tobacco sales (the Chinese state monopoly makes up 31 percent),[12] but the transnationals dominate international trade in tobacco, and control 70 percent of world production.[13]

The highest rates of cigarette consumption have shifted dramatically since the 1970s as the US tobacco corporations have increasingly turned to emerging regions for profits. In the early 1970s, cigarette consumption was highest in Western countries like Canada, Australia, the UK, and Switzerland. In the early 1990s, rates were highest in Poland, Greece, Hungary, Korea, and Japan—all of which have been targeted by Philip Morris or RJR Nabisco.[14]

Nearly 10,000 people around the world die every day from tobacco-related illnesses.[15] About one-third of the world's population aged 15 and over smokes, and the figures are increasing, especially in Asia, one of the key targets of the US tobacco corporations.[16] China has replaced the US as the country with the largest number of deaths from smoking. If current rates of smoking persist, tobacco will kill a third of all young men in China, half of them before the age of 70.[17] Consumption of cigarettes in China increased 260 percent between the early 1970s and the early 1990s, as the US tobacco giants established their presence and their brands in China.[18] Marlboro is among the ten most recognized consumer brands in China.[19]

While consumption of cigarettes in the US is declining by 1.5 percent per year, it is rising in developing countries by 1.7 percent annually. **Analysts expect international tobacco profits for the US tobacco giants to rise 20 percent annually for the next several years.**[20]

The international expansion by Philip Morris and RJR Nabisco amounts to a transfer of capital from economically poor countries to cash-rich corporations, and stockholders in wealthier countries.

The tobacco industry has fooled us in Africa. Money from some of the poorest nations in the world finds its way to the coffers of Europe and North America. We talk of famine and poverty plaguing Africa. Developed countries give us aid, then take our money from tobacco profits. They advertise with no regard for ethics or our welfare.—*Dr. Paul Wangai, Kenya Action on Smoking and Health*[21]

International tobacco market expansion has other costs: damage to the environment through deforestation, and world hunger as land needed for food production is converted to producing tobacco. Brazil and Zimbabwe surpassed the US as the largest exporters of tobacco leaf in 1994.[22] Brazil is also home to one of the world's largest rainforests,[23] and in Southern Africa, 12 percent of deforestation is due to tobacco.[24] A tremendous amount of wood is used in the tobacco curing process—one tree per 300 cigarettes—and land is cleared for tobacco production, all of which contributes to global deforestation.[25] Seventy-three percent of land dedicated to tobacco production is located in developing countries.[26] In Africa, most countries were once self-sustaining in food production. Land has been converted from food to tobacco production, the result being that developing countries that export tobacco are now importing food, such as Tanzania, Malawi, and Zimbabwe.[27] Worldwide, it is estimated that land taken by tobacco could produce food crops to feed 10-20 million people.[28] Ironically, Philip Morris widely advertises its anti-hunger philanthropy, which amounts to about $15-$20 million annually since 1990, or less than 0.5 percent of Philip Morris's $4 billion in profits from international tobacco sales in 1996.[29]

NOTES

1 "The Smoking Epidemic—'A Fire in the Global Village,'" World Health Organization press release, Aug. 25, 1997 (as presented by Dr. Richard Peto, Oxford University/World Health Organization Collaborating Centre for Chronic Disease Control at the 10th World Conference on Tobacco or Health, Beijing, Aug. 1997).

2 Philip Morris 1996 Annual Report, pp. 5, 11; "Fortune 500 Largest U.S. Corporations," *Fortune*, April 28, 1997, p. F-1.

3 Philip Morris 1996 Annual Report, p. 6; Tara Parker Pope, "Facts About the Global Tobacco Business," *Wall Street Journal*, June 23, 1997; "Leading Cigarette Brands Worldwide,"

World Market Share Reporter 1997-98, p. 86.

4   Philip Morris 1993 Annual Report, inside cover; Kurt Badenhausen, "Blind Faith," *Financial World*, July 8, 1996, p. 53.

5   "Fortune 500 Largest U.S. Corporations," *Fortune*, April 28, 1997, p. F-2.

6   "Global 500 Ranked Within Industries," *Fortune*, Aug. 4, 1997, pp. F-6, F-26.

7   Tara Parker Pope, "Facts About the Global Tobacco Business," *Wall Street Journal*, June 23, 1997; "Leading Cigarette Brands Worldwide," *World Market Share Reporter 1997-98*, p. 86.

8   "The 100 Largest U.S. Multinationals," *Forbes*, July 28, 1997, p. 219.

9   RJR Nabisco 1996 Annual Report, pp. 26, 30.

10   Nancy Stancill, "Teen-age Smoking Explodes Globally," *Charlotte Observer*, Oct. 20, 1997; Nancy Stancill, "Exporting Addiction?," *Charlotte Observer*, Oct. 18, 1997.

11   Jane Perlez, "Fenced In at Home, Marlboro Man Looks Abroad," *New York Times*, June 24, 1997.

12   World Health Organization Fact Sheet #118, "The Tobacco Epidemic: A Global Public Health Emergency," May 1996, p. 3.

13   Daya Kishan Thussu, "To Grow or Not to Grow, That is the Question," *Panos Features* (London: The Panos Institute, Sept. 30, 1994), pp. 1-2.

14   World Health Organization Fact Sheet #118, "The Tobacco Epidemic: A Global Public Health Emergency," May 1996, p. 2; Philip Morris Annual Report 1992, p. 17; Philip Morris Annual Report 1996, p. 10; RJR Nabisco Annual Report 1996, pp. 17, 20; Philip Morris 1982 Annual Report, p. 8; Philip Morris 1983 Annual Report, p. 6; Philip Morris 1987 Annual Report, p. 7; Philip Morris 1988 Annual Report, p. 11; R.J. Reynolds Annual Report 1983, p. 11.

15   "The Smoking Epidemic—'A Fire in the Global Village,'" World Health Organization press release, Aug. 25, 1997.

16 World Health Organization Fact Sheet #118, "The Tobacco Epidemic: A Global Public Health Emergency," May 1996, p. 1; RJR Nabisco Annual Report 1996, p. 20; Philip Morris 1992 Annual Report, p. 17.

17 "The Smoking Epidemic—'A Fire in the Global Village,'" World Health Organization press release, Aug. 25, 1997.

18 World Health Organization Fact Sheet #118, "The Tobacco Epidemic: A Global Public Health Emergency," May 1996, p. 1; Glenn Frankel and Steven Mufson, "Vast China Market Key to Smoking Disputes," *Washington Post*, Nov. 20, 1996, p. A01.

19 Laurence Zuckerman, "Chinese Noting Brands Especially from Japan," *New York Times*, Feb. 16, 1995 (SCARCNet summary).

20 Mike France, William Symonds, Monica Larner, Dave Lindorff, "The World War on Tobacco," *Business Week*, Nov. 11, 1996, p. 99.

21 Greg Connolly, "Global Expansion of the Transnational Tobacco Conglomerates," *Resisting Tobacco in Developing Countries* (Working Papers in Support of the 8th World Conference on Tobacco or Health), March 30-April 3, 1992, p. 10.

22 World Health Organization Fact Sheet #118, "The Tobacco Epidemic: A Global Public Health Emergency," May 1996, p. 3.

23 Brian Rajewski (Ed.), *Countries of the World*. (Detroit: Gale Research, 1998), p. 323.

24 H. Geist, "How Tobacco Farming Contributes to Tropical Deforestation," a paper presented to the National Committee for International Cooperation and Sustainable Development, Utrecht (Netherlands), Oct. 29, 1997, p. 7.

25 Simon Chapman and Wong Wai Leng, *Tobacco Control in the Third World: A Resource Atlas* (Penang: International Organization of Consumers Unions (IOCU), 1990), pp. 57-58, 120; Richard Tebere and Ogen Kevin Aliro, "Tobacco Taxes the Environment: An Introduction," *Uganda: Paying the Price of Growing Tobacco* (London: The Panos Institute, 1993), p. 1.

26 Simon Chapman and Wong Wai Leng, *Tobacco Control in the Third World: A Resource Atlas*. (Penang: International Organization of Consumers Unions (IOCU), 1990), p. 27.

27 Derek Yach, "The Impact of Smoking in Developing Countries with Special Reference to Africa," *International Journal of Health Services*, Vol. 16, No. 2, 1986, p. 288.

28 Michele Barry, "The Influence of the U.S. Tobacco Industry on the Health, Economy, and Environment of Developing Countries," *New England Journal of Medicine*, Vol. 324, No. 13, March 28, 1991, p. 918.

29 Chris Glass, "Making a Difference," *Tobacco Reporter,* Nov. 1997, p. 51; Philip Morris 1996 Annual Report, pp. 24, 56.

INFACT'S TOBACCO INDUSTRY CAMPAIGN

INFACT has a 21-year history of effective organizing to stop life-threatening abuses of transnational corporations (TNCs) and increase their accountability to people around the world. Perhaps best known for the successful Nestlé and GE Boycotts, INFACT launched its Tobacco Industry Campaign in 1993. The Campaign targets Philip Morris and RJR Nabisco, the two leading US-based tobacco transnationals. The goals of the Campaign are to stop the tobacco industry from addicting new customers around the world, especially children and young people, and to stop the tobacco industry from manipulating public policy in the interest of tobacco profits. A major strategy of the Campaign is INFACT's Tobacco Industry Boycott targeting Philip Morris's and RJR Nabisco's key food brands: Kraft, Post, Maxwell House, and Nabisco.

In April 1994, INFACT issued the following Public Challenge to the tobacco industry:

- Stop tobacco marketing and promotion that appeals to children and young people.
- Stop spreading tobacco addiction internationally.
- Stop influence over, and interference in, public policy on issues of tobacco and health.
- Stop deceiving people about the dangers of tobacco.
- Pay the high costs of health care associated with the tobacco epidemic.

Much progress remains to be made by the tobacco corporations in several of these areas, in particular on the international expansion by the tobacco transnationals (TTNs). As Philip Morris and RJR Nabisco face an increasingly hostile climate in the US in terms of litigation, regulation, and consumer pressure, and as rates of smoking decline in Western countries, economically poor countries are being even more heavily targeted to sustain the profits of the tobacco giants and their shareholders.

In 1997, the US tobacco corporations engaged in settlement negotiations with the attorneys general of 39 of the 40 states then suing the industry to recover some of the medical costs for treating people with tobacco-related illnesses (excluding Minnesota Attorney General Hubert Humphrey III).[1] These negotiations led to a proposal for federal legislation that would go beyond settling these state lawsuits, to include some voluntary advertising restrictions in exchange for vastly weakening the FDA's ability to regulate the industry. The deal would also provide immunity from future liability for the industry, including punitive damages, and it would allow the tobacco industry to keep documents secret that may contain information that could aid other countries in the fight against tobacco promotion.[2] The deal would virtually free the industry from liability in the US, and preserve the extremely profitable tobacco business largely due to international expansion and growth.[3]

> The settlement is not about the US, it is about the international community. The impact on the international community will be horrendous.—*Trish Fraser, ASH New Zealand*[4]

The US is in a position to help stop the global tobacco epidemic by prioritizing health standards over trade policy and applying the same standards as in the US to the operations of the US-based tobacco corporations in countries where standards are lower or nonexistent. The US can also help to ensure that international agencies have the necessary tools to hold the tobacco corporations accountable for their activities at home and abroad.

NOTES

1   Anthony Flint, "Tobacco Settlement Is No Done Deal, Chicago Talks Suggest," *Boston Globe*, May 29, 1997.

2   Anthony Flint, "Deal Is Reached in Tobacco Talks," *Boston*

Globe, June 21, 1997; prepared remarks of [Minnesota Attorney General] Hubert Humphrey III before the Koop/Kessler Advisory Committee, June 18, 1997 (from Action on Smoking and Health web site).

3   John R. Wilke and Jeffrey Taylor, "FTC Criticizes Proposed Tobacco Accord," *Wall Street Journal*, Sept. 23, 1997, and Barnaby Feder, "The Ability to Turn a Profit Is Greater Than Deal's Cost," *New York Times*, June 21, 1997.

4   Response to INFACT survey from the 10th World Conference on Tobacco or Health, Beijing, Aug. 1997.

FINANCIAL BACKGROUND OF THE US-BASED TOBACCO CORPORATIONS: PHILIP MORRIS AND RJR NABISCO

Many of us at some point have internalized the tobacco industry's public relations message that people "choose" death by tobacco, and therefore we have blamed individual smokers for making themselves sick, or making us sick, rather than looking at the corporate root of this epidemic.

The dazzling success of Philip Morris and RJR Nabisco at marketing and promoting an addictive and deadly product has generated massive profits for these corporations at the expense of the health and lives of millions around the world. Those profits, in turn, have enabled the US-based tobacco transnationals to command undue influence over public policy, and the social and cultural climate, in the US and around the world.

The influence these giants can wield is not surprising given their size in comparison to many of the countries in which they operate. Philip Morris and RJR Nabisco had revenues in 1996 that far exceeded the Gross Domestic Product (GDP) of many countries. RJR Nabisco has revenues of $17 billion, exceeding the 1994 GDP of Costa Rica, Croatia, Cuba, El Salvador, Lebanon, or Jamaica. Philip Morris, with $55 billion in revenues in 1996, is larger than the GDP of Ecuador, Guatemala, Kenya, Kuwait, Malaysia, or Peru. Philip Morris's size is roughly equivalent to the economies of Ireland, Singapore, or Hungary.[1]

The overall revenues of Philip Morris and RJR Nabisco are increasingly dependent on international tobacco sales, as demonstrated below.

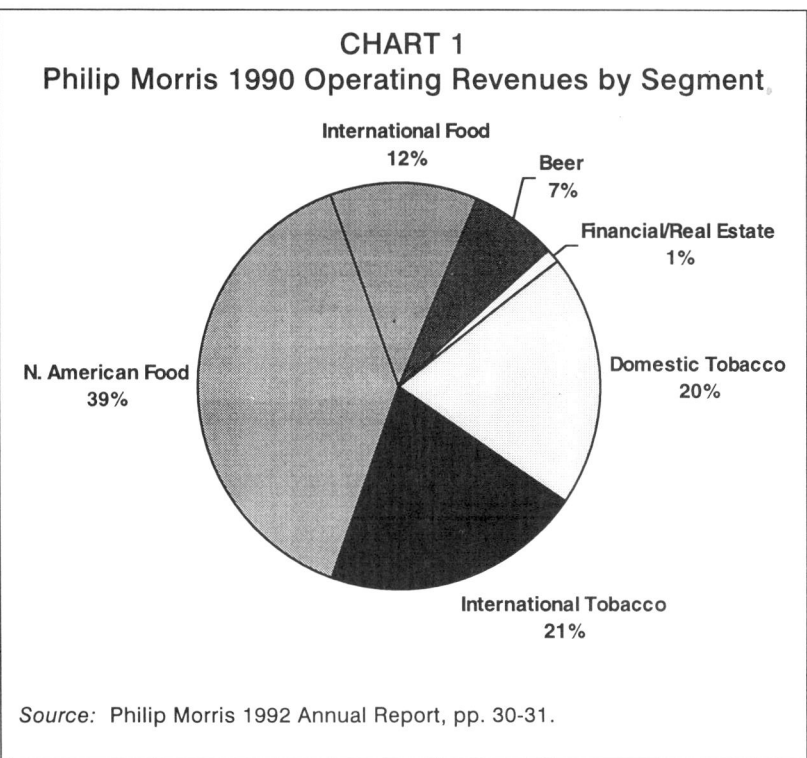

CHART 1
Philip Morris 1990 Operating Revenues by Segment

International Food 12%

Beer 7%

Financial/Real Estate 1%

N. American Food 39%

Domestic Tobacco 20%

International Tobacco 21%

Source: Philip Morris 1992 Annual Report, pp. 30-31.

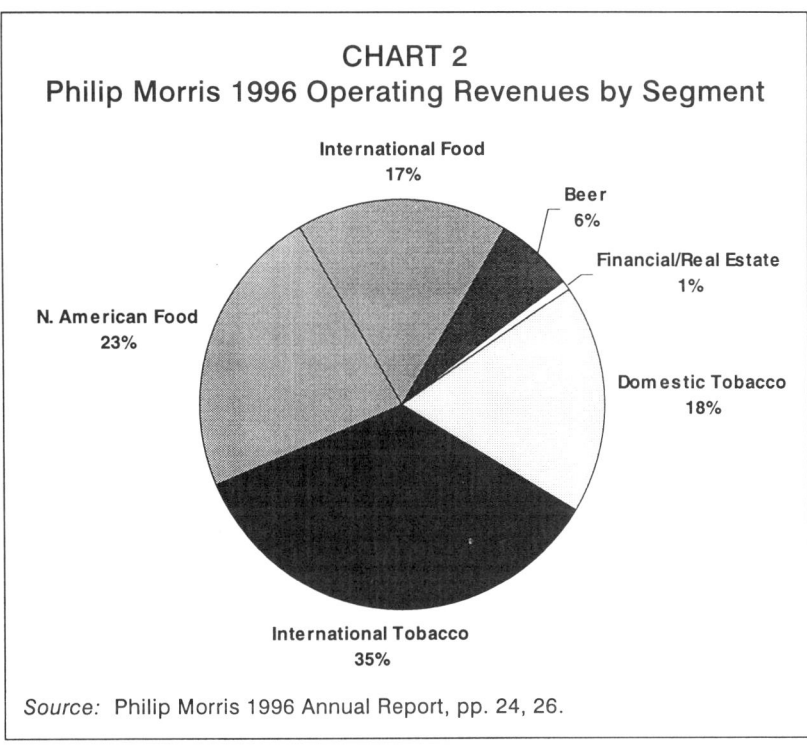

CHART 2
Philip Morris 1996 Operating Revenues by Segment

International Food 17%

Beer 6%

Financial/Real Estate 1%

N. American Food 23%

Domestic Tobacco 18%

International Tobacco 35%

Source: Philip Morris 1996 Annual Report, pp. 24, 26.

Philip Morris is ranked #6 among US-based corporations in profits.[2] In 1993, Philip Morris derived 61 percent of its tobacco sales from international markets. This figure rose to 66 percent by 1996.[3]

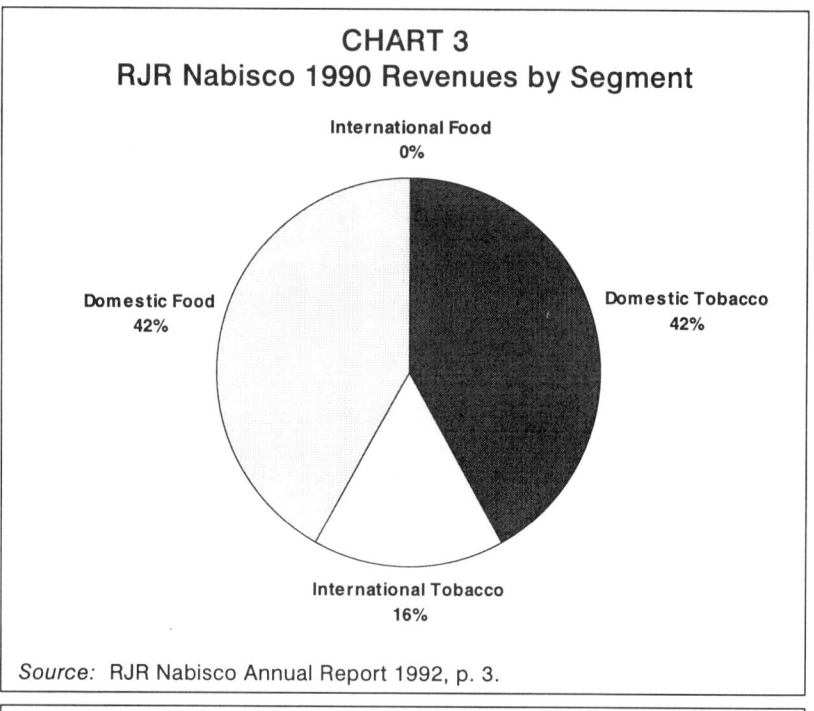

CHART 3
RJR Nabisco 1990 Revenues by Segment

International Food
0%

Domestic Food
42%

Domestic Tobacco
42%

International Tobacco
16%

Source: RJR Nabisco Annual Report 1992, p. 3.

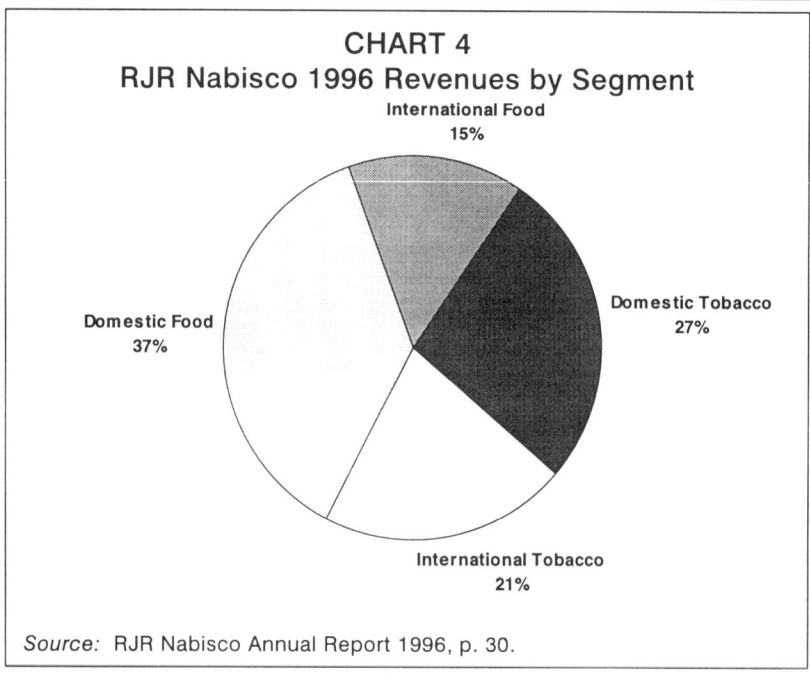

CHART 4
RJR Nabisco 1996 Revenues by Segment

International Food
15%

Domestic Food
37%

Domestic Tobacco
27%

International Tobacco
21%

Source: RJR Nabisco Annual Report 1996, p. 30.

Through tactics, such as joint ventures, investing in state-owned tobacco companies in China and Russia, direct acquisitions, installing people on their boards with key political or economic connections, licensing out tobacco brands for non-tobacco products, advertising and promotion, and hiring high-powered political consultants, the US-based tobacco transnationals expand their empire.

RJR Nabisco sells tobacco in more than 170 markets. Philip Morris is pushing its tobacco in 180 markets.[4] International tobacco sales for Philip Morris have risen 53 percent since 1993 and profits have increased 73 percent, while RJR Nabisco's profits from international tobacco sales have jumped 84 percent since 1993.[5] International tobacco sales for Philip Morris and RJR Nabisco have quadrupled in the past decade, while domestic sales have stagnated.[6]

Philip Morris owns or leases 47 international cigarette-manufacturing plants, while RJR Nabisco has 20 cigarette plants outside the US.[7]

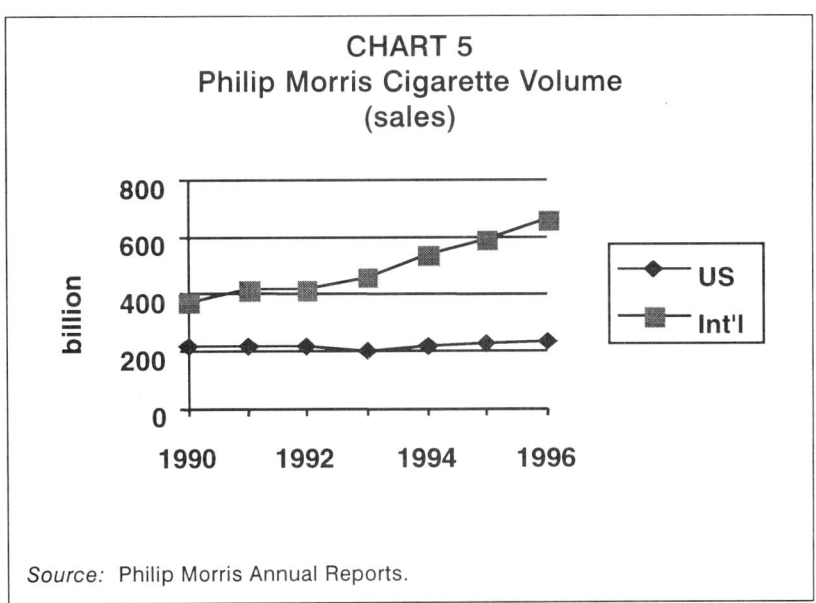

CHART 5
Philip Morris Cigarette Volume
(sales)

Source: Philip Morris Annual Reports.

TABLE I
Philip Morris and RJR Nabisco
Cigarette Market Share:
Selected Countries

Country	Philip Morris Market Share (1996)	RJR Nabisco Market Share (1996)	# Tobacco-Related Deaths Annually
Argentina	61%	N/A	†14,000
Austria	27%	N/A	8,000
Belgium	34%	6%	15,000
Brazil	15%	0%	N/A
Czech Republic	85%	<5%	22,700
France	30%	N/A	55,000
Germany	41%	N/A	110,000
Greece	23%	N/A	†10,000
Hong Kong	57%	N/A	N/A
Hungary	30%	<6%(est.)	34,000
Italy	54%	2%	81,000
Japan	17%	N/A	90,234
Korea	6%	N/A	N/A
Malaysia	10%	18%	N/A
Mexico	17%*	N/A	N/A
Morocco	63%	34%	N/A
Netherlands	32%	14%	25,100
Philippines	25%	N/A	9,885 (cancer only)
Portugal	24%	1%	8,400
Puerto Rico	37%	49%	N/A
Romania	17%	15%	28,500
Russia	34%	21%	280,000
Singapore	41%	21%	2,500
Slovak Republic	49%	<1% (est.)	9,500
Spain	22%	12%	†46,000
Sweden	17%	N/A	7,100
Switzerland	46%	9%	6,800
Turkey	19%	4%	N/A
Ukraine	14%	16%	107,000
UK	6%	2%	123,000
US	48%	25%	529,000
Venezuela	23%	0%	1,434

* Marlboro brand only.   †Males only.

Sources: Philip Morris 1996 Annual Report, p. 11; Tobacco International, June 1997, Sept. 1997, Nov. 1997; Tobacco Reporter, Oct. 1997, pp. 30-32; International Agency on Tobacco and Health, Oct. 1997 (Romania); World Health Organization (death statistics), "Tobacco or Health: A Global Status Report," 1997; Maxwell, John C., Market Up, April 1997, cited in "FTC Criticizes Proposed Tobacco Accord," Wall Street Journal, Sept. 23, 1997, p.A1; Business in Russia, Feb. 1997, p.75, cited in World Market Share Reporter, 1997-98, p.86; Philippine Cancer Society web site; Peto, Richard, et.al., Mortality from Smoking in Developed Countries 1950-2000. Oxford: Oxford University Press, 1994, pp.119, 392; Ukraine State Statistics Committee (Ukraine market share data).

NOTE: Data from China is incomplete, and therefore not included. China has overtaken the US in the number of annual tobacco-related deaths.

TABLE II
Top Five Cigarette Markets Worldwide —1996

Country	Cigarettes Sold (billions)	% of Population That Smokes
China	1,791	61% (males); 7% (females)
United States	488	27% (males); 23% (females)
Japan	335	59% (males); 15% (females)
Russia	180	67% (males); 25-30% (females)
Indonesia	173	60% (males); 5% (females)

Source: "Facts About the Global Tobacco Business," *Wall Street Journal,* June 23, 1997; World Health Organization Tobacco or Health Programme, "Tobacco or Health: A Global Status Report," 1997 (prevalence data).

NOTES

1   Otto Johnson (Ed.), *Information Please Almanac, Atlas and Yearbook.* (New York: Houghton Mifflin, 1997), pp. 171, 172, 173, 182, 221, 212, 179, 198, 216, 219, 228, 248, 209, 261, 201.

2   "The Leaders in 1997 Sales and Profits," *Business Week*, March 2, 1998, p. 110.

3   Philip Morris 1993 Annual Report, p. 22; Philip Morris 1996 Annual Report, p. 24.

4   RJR Nabisco 1996 10-K, p. 3; Philip Morris 1993 Annual Report, p. 3.

5   Philip Morris 1993 Annual Report, p. 22; Philip Morris 1996 Annual Report, p. 24; RJR Nabisco 1993 Annual Report, p. 27; RJR Nabisco 1996 Annual Report, p. 30.

6   Anthony Flint (Boston Globe), "U.S. Tobacco Giants Focus on Exports," *Salisbury Post* (Maryland), Sept. 8, 1996.

7   Nancy Stancill, "Carolinas Flavor Moves Overseas," *Charlotte Observer*, posted Oct. 18, 1997 (from internet).

THE INFLUENCE OF PHILIP MORRIS AND RJR NABISCO IN TRADE POLICY

In the 1980s, the US Trade Representative helped to force open markets of Japan, South Korea, Taiwan, and Thailand for the US tobacco corporations, and challenged those countries' health measures on tobacco as unfair trade barriers using section 301 of the Trade Act of 1974.[1] US-based transnationals then introduced very sophisticated and extremely effective advertising and promotion techniques along with their deadly product. The competition drove formerly lethargic national companies to adopt aggressive new marketing tactics in response to the US corporations. The results have been devastating for human health. Since the entry of the US tobacco corporations, smoking rates in each of these countries have risen dramatically.

In Japan, cigarette ads rose from fortieth to second place in total television air time in just one year following the entry of the US tobacco giants in 1987; two-thirds of the ads were for US brands.[2] An average of 60 ads for US tobacco brands were appearing per day on Japanese TV by the early 1990s, many of them during programs watched by teenagers.[3] The total consumption of cigarettes in Japan, Taiwan, and Korea increased 11 percent between 1986 and 1989.[4] Between 1987 and 1993, cigarette consumption by teens in Japan increased 16 percent.[5] From 1990-1996, smoking among 17-year-olds in Japan climbed from 26 to 40 percent for boys and 5 to 15 percent among girls.[6] By 1989, US tobacco transnational exports to Japan had nearly quintupled since 1986; cigarette advertising expenditures tripled in the two years after the US forced open the Japanese market.[7]

Foreign tobacco corporations were credited with essentially introducing cigarette advertising into Taiwan when they gained access to the market in 1986, and advertising and promotional expenditures for the Korean national tobacco monopoly skyrocketed 641 percent between 1987 and 1990 after US cigarettes became some of the most heavily advertised products in the country in 1988.[8]

The smoking rate among Taiwanese high school students jumped from 22 percent the year before the US corporations entered the market to 32 percent two years later.[9] Smoking rates among male Korean teenagers rose from 18 percent to 30 percent in one year after import restrictions were removed, and the rate among female teens rose from less than 2 percent to 9 percent—an increase of greater than 400 percent.[10] Between 1988 and 1991, the number of Thai smokers between the ages of 15 and 19 rose 24 percent.[11]

During the Clinton Administration, the US has stopped the aggressive use of section 301 of the Trade Act of 1974 to overturn laws in other countries designed to protect public health, and to force open markets on behalf of the US tobacco corporations. The US government has taken initial steps to desist aiding the US tobacco corporations in their expansion into international markets. In 1997, Congress passed legislation that temporarily prohibits federal trade officials from promoting US tobacco exports. The legislation also prevents the US Trade Representative, State and Commerce departments from trying to weaken other countries' restrictions designed to limit tobacco sales in the interest of public health,[12] and efforts are underway to make the changes permanent.[13] Yet Philip Morris and RJR Nabisco have found other ways to favorably influence trade policy for the US tobacco industry.

The US-based Tobacco Giants and the Multilateral Agreement on Investment (MAI)

Philip Morris and RJR Nabisco are involved in several trade associations, front groups, and negotiating committees advising the US State Department, the US Trade Representative, and President Clinton on the MAI treaty, and other trade agreements.[14] Through their trade associations and front groups,[15] Philip Morris and RJR Nabisco were part of a corporate coalition called America Leads on Trade which pushed "fast track" legislation in 1997 that would give President Clinton the authority to sign trade agreements that the US Congress would vote for or against but would not be able to amend. The coalition said more than $5 million was spent by Big

Business on the campaign.[16] The timing of the legislation coincided with the expansion of the North American Free Trade Agreement and the secretive but very important negotiations around the Multilateral Agreement on Investment (MAI), a treaty designed to loosen foreign investment and regulatory restrictions on transnational corporations.

Philip Morris and RJR Nabisco have representatives on two business associations directly involved in the MAI negotiations: the United States Council for International Business (USCIB), and the Business and Industry Advisory Council (BIAC) of the Organization for Economic Cooperation and Development (OECD). The USCIB lobbies on behalf of US business interests on trade and investment policy, and is a member of the BIAC.[17] The OECD is the international body through which the MAI is being negotiated, initially in secret. The potential benefits to Philip Morris and RJR Nabisco of the MAI are enormous. The corporations could challenge health regulations, and even sue governments directly for loss of future profits related to such regulations. Because of the intense public outcry in the US and other countries when a draft text was leaked, the prospects for the treaty are uncertain, but its key provisions are likely to turn up in other international forums if it is abandoned within OECD.[18]

John F. Manfredi, Executive Vice President of Corporate Affairs for Nabisco, Inc., and William H. Webb, President and CEO of Philip Morris International, Inc., are on the Board of Trustees of the USCIB. Hugh Cullman, former Vice Chair of Philip Morris Companies, Inc., is a Senior Trustee of USCIB, and Wendy Burrell, Director of Public Affairs at Philip Morris International, Inc., serves as Vice Chair of the Marketing, Advertising and Distribution Committee of the Council. Manfredi (Nabisco) and Webb (Philip Morris) are on the Executive Committee of USCIB.[19]

The CEO of Philip Morris and a high-level representative of RJR Nabisco are members of the very influential Business Roundtable, made up of CEOs of many of the largest US corporations.[20] The Business Roundtable has enormous access and influence on policy issues in Washington.

While current political rhetoric is "anti-Big Government," not enough of us recognize or are indignant about transnational corporations having greater control over our lives. In fact, the tobacco corporations manipulate anti-government and anti-regulatory sentiment to avoid accountability for their actions, even as they oppose policies supported by the majority of the public.

PROVISIONS OF THE MAI WITH SIGNIFICANT IMPLICATIONS FOR THE CONTROL OF THE INTERNATIONAL EXPANSION OF THE TRANSNATIONAL TOBACCO CORPORATIONS

• *Elimination of special treatment for national companies.* Home countries would no longer be allowed to give special consideration to national companies or apply restrictions on foreign ownership and investment.[21] This provision could have particular implications regarding the tax status of the US tobacco transnationals in other countries. Philip Morris, for example, could claim a violation of the MAI if a signatory to the treaty applies different tax rates to national companies. In addition, the MAI would ban performance requirements for TNCs to qualify for tax incentives or government subsidies.

This would make it virtually impossible for many national companies in Asia, Eastern Europe, and the former Soviet Republics to compete, and therefore, make them more likely to be purchased at bargain prices by the tobacco giants, Philip Morris and RJR Nabisco.

• *Compensation for expropriated assets.* This provision says any government seizure "tantamount to expropriation" must be compensated.[22] Thus, compensation could apply to assets and future profits not actually expropriated, but lost due to government regulations, including tobacco control measures. In the case of the tobacco transnationals, they could sue for compensation for any regulation that would affect future earnings, including the proposed settlement legislation in the US, or even local ordinances.

• *TNCs could sue governments directly.* The MAI would essentially set up a dispute resolution mechanism in which governments and corporations are equal players. The treaty would establish an international tribunal where corporations can sue countries for policies that "violate" investor "rights." However, governments could not sue corporations for investments that cause harm to their countries.[23] This could have serious implications for countries seeking compensation from the tobacco corporations for medical costs arising from tobacco-related illnesses.

• *"Roll back" and "Standstill" provision on regulations.* This provision would void national and local laws that conflict with rules agreed upon in the MAI. Future laws are also forbidden which conflict with this agreement, although countries could exempt a number of existing laws.[24] This provision could be an impediment to future tobacco control legislation, and it has serious implications for the World Health Organization's efforts to establish an International Framework Convention for tobacco control (i.e., some international standards in the form of a treaty).

NOTES

1   "Trade and Health Issues: Dichotomy Between U.S. Tobacco
    Export Policy and Antismoking Initiatives," US General Ac-
    counting Office (GAO), May 1990, p. 11.

2   Stephen R. Shalom, "Made in the USA: Deadly Exports," *Z
    Magazine*, April 1992, p. 19; Gale Eisenstodt and Hiroko
    Katayama, "A Trade Threat that Worked," *Forbes*, April 3,
    1989; Glenn Frankel, "U.S. Aided Cigarette Firms In Conquests
    Across Asia," *Washington Post*, Nov. 17, 1996.

3   William Ecenbarger, "America's New Merchants of Death,"
    Reader's Digest, April 1993, p. 53.

4   Morton Mintz, "Tobacco Roads: Delivering Death to the Third
    World," *The Progressive*, May 1991, p. 28.

5   William Ecenbarger, "America's New Merchants of Death,"
    Reader's Digest, April 1993, p. 57.

6   Nancy Stancill, "Exporting Addiction?," *Charlotte Observer*,
    Oct. 18, 1997.

7   Gale Eisenstodt and Hiroko Katayama, "A Trade Threat that
    Worked," *Forbes*, April 3, 1989.

8   "Background Information on US Efforts to Force Thailand to
    Import and Advertise US Cigarettes," The American Cancer
    Society, Feb. 5, 1990; Morton Mintz, "Tobacco Roads: Deliv-
    ering Death to the Third World," *The Progressive*, May 1991,
    pp. 28-29; "International Trade: Advertising and Promoting US
    Cigarettes in Selected Asian Countries," US General Account-
    ing Office (GAO), Dec. 1992, p. 67.

9   Morton Mintz, "Tobacco Roads: Delivering Death to the Third
    World," *The Progressive*, May 1991, p. 29.

10 "Trade and Health Issues: Dichotomy Between US Tobacco
    Export Policy and Antismoking Initiatives," May 1990, US
    General Accounting Office (GAO), p. 31.

11 William Ecenbarger, "America's New Merchants of Death,"
    Reader's Digest, April 1993, p. 57.

12 "House Votes End to Tobacco Boost," *Boston Globe*, Sept. 27,
    1997; Bill Summary & Status for the 105th Congress, from gov-

ernment web site (thomas.loc.gov). The bill was signed into law Nov. 26, 1997.

13 "Durbin, Colleagues Propose International Tobacco Protocol as Part of Tobacco Legislation, press release from Senator Dick Durbin (IL), Feb. 26, 1998.

14 United States Council for International Business membership list, January 1998 (from USCIB web site); John Canham-Clyne, "Following the Money," *Public Citizen*, Fall 1996, p. 16; *Associations Yellow Book* (Leadership Directories Inc., Summer 1997), p. 354.

15 America Leads on Trade membership list, 1997; John Canham-Clyne, "Following the Money," *Public Citizen*, Fall 1996, p. 16; *Associations Yellow Book* (Leadership Directories Inc., Summer 1997), p. 354.

16 "Costly Track," *Wall Street Journal*, Nov. 7, 1997.

17 United States Council for International Business membership list, January 1998 (from USCIB web site); Business and Industry Advisory Council Annual Report 1996, p. 6.

18 "Investing Abroad Made Safer?," *Fortune*, Jan. 12, 1998, p. 46; US Council on International Business Statement on Administration's Proposal on Fast Track (from USCIB web site, Oct. 3, 1997); Business and Industry Advisory Council Annual Report 1996, p. 12; "The MAI Negotiating Text," OECD, Feb. 14, 1998; "The Multilateral Agreement on Investment: Key Provisions," (fact sheet) The Preamble Center for Public Policy, 1997. Ward Morehouse, "The Multilateral Agreement on Investment: An International Human Rights Crisis: Reflections on Next Steps and a Call to Action" (New York: Program on Corporations, Law and Democracy, A Work in Progress, December 1997).

19 United States Council for International Business web site, Feb. 27, 1998.

20 *Associations Yellow Book* (Leadership Directories, Inc., Summer 1997), pp. 353-354; Hilary Stout and Laurie McGinley, "Tax Break Cap On Health Plan Gains Support," *Wall Street Journal*, Dec. 16, 1992 (SCARCNet Summary).

21 "The MAI Negotiating Text," OECD, Feb. 14, 1998, p. 13; "The Multilateral Agreement on Investment: Key Provisions," (fact

sheet) The Preamble Center for Public Policy, 1997.

22 "The Multilateral Agreement on Investment: Key Provisions," (fact sheet) The Preamble Center for Public Policy, 1997; "The MAI Negotiating Text," OECD, Feb. 14, 1998, pp. 52-57.

23 "The Multilateral Agreement on Investment: Key Provisions," (fact sheet) The Preamble Center for Public Policy, 1997; "The MAI Negotiating Text," OECD, Feb. 14, 1998, pp. 58-81.

24 "The MAI Negotiating Text," OECD, Feb. 14, 1998, pp. 18-21; "The Multilateral Agreement on Investment: Key Provisions," (fact sheet) The Preamble Center for Public Policy, 1997.

CORPORATE MARKETING AND PROMOTION OF TOBACCO BRANDS: KEY TO INTERNATIONAL EXPANSION

The marketing sophistication and large advertising budgets of the tobacco transnationals guarantee their position in the world market. **Philip Morris is among the world's top ten advertising spenders.** Philip Morris spent over $3 billion ($813 million outside the US) worldwide in advertising in 1996, and ranked ninth among leading advertisers in the world. This figure includes both food and tobacco advertising. By comparison, B.A.T was ranked 44th, and spent $421 million worldwide.[1] Philip Morris's ad spending outside the US has increased by 72 percent since 1990.[2] Philip Morris was among the top 25 advertisers in print media based on Marlboro advertising alone in Europe, Asia, and Latin America in 1996.[3] Philip Morris's international advertising expenditures do not include all promotions (non-media). Advertising is paid media, such as ads in magazines, billboards, TV, and radio. Promotions include cigarette giveaways, sports sponsorships, and contests.[4] Advertising spending also goes much further in economically poor countries.

The tobacco transnationals rely on the US as a base of political power and legitimacy, as well as a cultural base for associating all that is envied and admired about the US with their product. The tobacco industry taps into the deeply held notion that no one should tell an individual what to do—even as they design advertisements to influence individuals to purchase an addictive product.

The US-based tobacco corporations capitalize on the appeal of American products, Western cultural themes and images of wealth, leisure, and freedom. In a Camel billboard advertisement in Senegal, the phrase "Made in the USA" is the message under the Camel

logo. An observer noted most of the people appearing in US tobacco corporation ads in Senegal are Caucasian.[5]

A Marlboro booth inside a typical general food store in St. Louis, Senegal.
Posters for Philip Morris's Marlboro and L&M brands outside the store
promote a chance to win a Ford Mustang, or a trip to the US. Photo by
Anna White, 1997.

This Camel ad in Senegal boasts that the brand is "Made in the USA."
Photo by Anna White, 1996.

The issues around advertising and promotion of tobacco are more complex when one considers that the industry is selling and promoting more than cigarettes. By relying on themes of freedom, wealth and luxury, the tobacco corporations promote a set of social norms and values in which cigarette smoking figures prominently. In essence, the tobacco corporations are marketing US culture and a culture of consumption. In this context, the targeting of economically poor nations takes on new significance. The illusion of power, wealth, and independence associated with cigarettes in the ads becomes all the more insidious. The tobacco transnationals tap into the aspirations of people living in targeted countries where populations are beginning to have some disposable income, by selling not just cigarettes but a Western standard of living, freedom, and democracy. These messages are filled with irony, such as identifying freedom with an addictive product.

An ad attached to an airline ticket stub in the Czech Republic uses American icons to sell Philip Morris's *Super Lights, American Blend.* The Statue of Liberty, draped in the American flag, selling death and disease.[6]

Until the arrival of the transnational tobacco companies and the beginning of aggressive advertising, the prevalence of smoking was decreasing. — *Dr. Jiri T. Kozak, an adviser to the Czech Ministry of Health.*[7]

In Russia, the US tobacco giants promote cigarettes as part of the Western lifestyle. Philip Morris's L&M advertises "A date with America" in a popular youth publication, featuring young people in leather jackets and jeans next to a Harley-Davidson motorcycle. Among 13-to-16-year-old Russians, smoking rates increased from 31.5 percent to 42.5 percent from 1992 to 1993.[8]

MINISTR ZDRAVOTNICTVÍ VARUJE. KOUŘENÍ ZPŮSOBUJE RAKOVINU.

Philip Morris uses popular American culture and images of wealth and leisure in promotions like this Harley-Davidson motorcycle giveaway in popular youth publications and brochures in Russia and Eastern Europe. This 1997 L&M ad uses the phrase "a symbol of freedom."[9]

TABLE III Countries In Which Philip Morris Is a Top Ten Advertiser (in millions)		
Country	Philip Morris Ad Spending 1996	Rank Among Top Advertisers
Austria	$17.5	9
Belgium	$28.3	6
Bulgaria	$1.2	3
Canada	$3.2	5
Czech Republic	$3.3	9
France	$128.5	7
Germany	$207.2	10
Hong Kong	$12.9	9
Indonesia	$6.3	10
Kuwait	$3.9	1
Oman	$0.6	5
Qatar	$0.3	9
Romania	$2.1	4
Saudi Arabia	$3.4	3
Slovak Republic	$1.8	3
Sweden	$31.2	7
Switzerland	$26.2	4
United States	$2,278.0	3

Source: Advertising Age International, Nov. 1997, pp. 9-12.
Note: These figures include food and tobacco advertising.

As indicated in the table above, Philip Morris is spending enormous sums on advertising even in countries where advertising restrictions are in place. For example, in France Philip Morris spent more than $128 million in 1996, though there is a ban on most forms of direct tobacco advertising except point-of-sale,[10] indicating the tobacco corporation is finding new ways to market and promote its products. Tobacco ad spending is still high in places like Norway, Finland, and other countries with advertising restrictions because spending is often shifted or increased for sports and event sponsorship, or other indirect tobacco promotion.

Likewise, in Malaysia where RJR Nabisco is the fourth leading advertiser ($9.5 million on media in 1996), there is a ban on most forms of direct cigarette advertising, except at the point of sale and sponsorships.[11] RJR Nabisco instead promotes tobacco brand names on non-tobacco items, a practice known as "brand stretching."[12]

The Failure of Corporate Self-Regulation

The US tobacco corporations have a history of routinely violating their own voluntary Cigarette Advertising and Promotion Code adopted in 1964 and revised most recently in 1990. The enforcement provisions of the Code, which included fines of $100,000 for a violation, were eliminated in 1970.[13] The US tobacco giants never intended to apply the Code to their international tobacco operations, a clear signal of the need for global tobacco control standards. In fact, the corporations insist the Code applies only in the US, and that criticism of its marketing in developing countries is paternalistic.[14] The industry's Code, the source of which is the Tobacco Institute, includes the following:

- No one depicted in cigarette advertising shall be or appear to be under 25 years of age.

Young people pictured on the cover of a Marlboro Red Hot Hits CD from Hong Kong, a form of "brand stretching." All appear to be under the age of 25.[15]

- Cigarette advertising shall not appear on billboards located within 500 feet of any elementary school, junior high school, or high school or any children's playground.

Posters for the Camel Planet club are plastered outside an elementary school in Poland. The Camel Planet nightclub is just a short distance away. A Camel kiosk sells cigarettes just outside a high school.[16] Photos by Scott Thompson, 1996.

- Cigarette advertising shall not suggest that smoking is essential to social prominence, distinction, success or sexual attraction; nor shall it picture a person smoking in an exaggerated manner.

Sex and exaggeration in one widely used US advertisement for RJR Nabisco's Camel. The camel can be made out in the smoke ring.[17]

- Cigarette advertising shall not depict as a smoker anyone who is or has been well known as an athlete, nor shall it show any smoker participating in, or obviously just having participated in, a physical activity requiring stamina or athletic conditioning beyond that of normal recreation.

Philip Morris and RJR Nabisco ads frequently associate smoking with strenuous and athletic activity in violation of the industry marketing code. This 1998 Marlboro Unlimited gear brochure from the US features a mountain biker, and the 1997 Camel ad from the Czech Republic produced by ad agency McCann-Erickson uses whitewater rafters.[18]

- Persons who engage in sampling shall refuse to give a sample to any person whom they know to be under 21 years of age or who, without reasonable identification to the contrary, appears to be less than 21 years of age.

Young girls in Cambodia handing out free cigarettes.[19] This type of promotion illustrates Philip Morris's willingness not just to target children and young people with advertising, but to exploit them in promoting tobacco internationally. When Philip Morris CEO Geoffrey Bible was confronted with this photo at US Congressional hearings in January 1998, he said he "would control that as best I can."[20]

- Sampling shall not be conducted in or on public streets, sidewalks or parks, except in places that are open only to persons to whom cigarettes lawfully may be sold.

- There shall be no other distribution of non-tobacco premium items bearing cigarette brand names, logos, etc. except with the purchase of a package or carton of cigarettes or to persons 21 years of age or older.

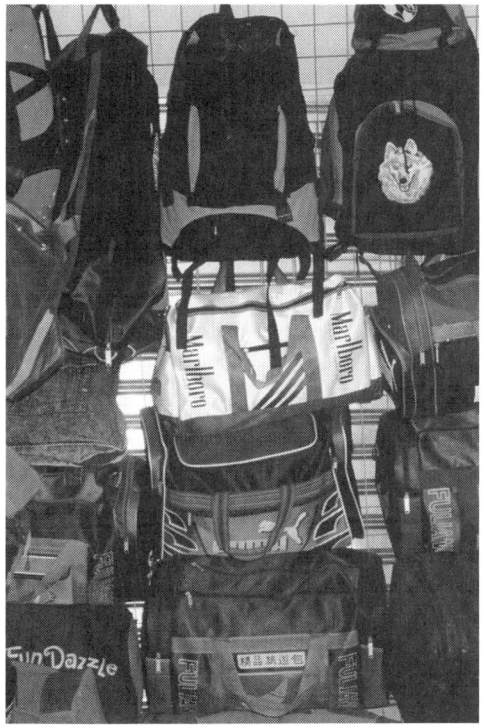

Marlboro athletic bags on sale in stores around Beijing in 1997. Photos by INFACT.[21]

- Clothing bearing cigarette brand names or logos shall be in adult sizes only.

Man holding child-size Marlboro T-shirt in Kenya. [22]

The fact that the US tobacco corporations have ignored their own voluntary advertising code demonstrates the need for independent regulations and enforcement.

At US Congressional hearings in 1998, the CEOs of the five major US tobacco corporations, including Philip Morris and RJR Nabisco, were asked to take a pledge to immediately cease marketing and advertising that encourages children overseas to smoke. None took the pledge.[23] The CEO of Brown & Williamson said that in Japan his corporation follows the voluntary marketing code developed by the Tobacco Institute of Japan (TIOJ).[24] However, this code is also routinely violated, according to local tobacco control activists. The Japanese Code states that no advertising or sales promotions will be directed toward minors, but the tobacco corporations advertise in magazines popular among young people. The transnationals also distribute free cigarettes on the streets, at concerts and restaurants frequented by teenagers.[25]

HIDING BEHIND CHEESE AND CEREAL: KRAFT'S ROLE IN PROMOTING TOBACCO

The US-based tobacco corporations began expanding into the food business in the 1970s. The wholesome image of Philip Morris's Kraft and RJR's Nabisco divisions provides respectability and legitimacy for their tobacco operations. Their food divisions also give them greater leverage politically and economically. In 1994, Philip Morris sued the ABC television network for a program it had aired on boosting nicotine levels in cigarettes, and according to *Advertising Age International,* threatened to pull $100 million of its Kraft Foods and Miller beer advertising from the network.[26]

In 1996 and 1997, well-paid lobbyists from Kraft's Washington, DC-based firm Olsson, Frank and Weeda, and also from Black, Kelly, Scruggs and Healey (which lobbies on food and tobacco for Philip Morris), lobbied for FDA "reform."[27] Original versions of the bill which passed in 1997 would have affected the FDA's ability to regulate the tobacco industry.[28]

In 1995, after the US FDA announced its intention to regulate the tobacco industry, Philip Morris mobilized its Oscar Mayer employees to write letters opposing the FDA regulations.[29] During the 1996 US federal elections, Democrats largely attempted to distance themselves from the tobacco industry. However, Philip Morris's Kraft, as a vice chair of the host committee, contributed at least $100,000 in soft money to the Chicago convention. Kraft and Miller sponsored events at the Democratic National Convention.[30]

Marlboro and Kraft products are frequently seen promoted together. The same advertising agency, Dentsu, Young & Rubicam, is responsible for Philip Morris's Kraft Foods International and tobacco advertising in China.[31] Photo by INFACT, Beijing, Aug. 1997.

Many of the same advertising agencies used to promote Philip Morris's international tobacco business also promote Philip Morris-owned Kraft Foods (see chart, below). These are the leading advertising agencies in the world, and many are among the ten biggest firms[32]—the best money can buy.

TABLE IV
Philip Morris and RJR Nabisco International Advertising Agencies

Advertising Agency	World Rank	Philip Morris (Tobacco)	Kraft Foods	RJR Nabisco (Tobacco)	RJR Nabisco (Food)
Ammirati Puris Lintas	#15			X	
BBDO Worldwide	#5		X		
Dentsu Young & Rubicam	#1	X	X		
FCA! BMZ Int'l	N/A				X
FCB	#10				X
Grey Advertising	#8		X		
J. Walter Thompson Co.	#3	X	X		
Leo Burnett Co.	#6	X	X		
McCann-Erickson Worldwide	#2			X	X
Ogilvy & Mather Worldwide	#9	X	X		
Saatchi & Saatchi Advertising Worldwide	#11	X			
TBWA International	#18	X			
Young & Rubicam	#16		X		

Source: Advertising Age International, Sept. 1997, pp. i11, i18, i20-24, i28-i31, i50, Advertising Age, April 15, 1996, p. s15.

Leo Burnett, the advertising firm that created the Marlboro Man campaign, has also conducted public relations campaigns to undermine public health policies outside the US. In the Philippines, Leo Burnett devised a public relations strategy for Philip Morris for the purpose of undermining cancer awareness and prevention programs as a public health priority, though that particular proposal was ultimately rejected, according to the New York Times.[33]

Getting Around Advertising Bans and Restrictions

Many countries are considering or have enacted laws restricting tobacco ads, including Mexico, Latvia, Brazil, and Belgium.[34] Other countries already have advertising and promotion restrictions in place that far surpass current US laws, such as Australia, Thailand, Singapore, Finland, Canada, and Mongolia.[35]

In 1990, 27 countries had total or near-total bans on advertising. However, this number had dropped to just 18 in 1996.[36] By late 1997, about 30 countries placed some restrictions on tobacco advertising.[37]

Over 100 countries have bans on tobacco television advertisements, approximately 90 have bans on radio ads, 66 countries have banned advertising in cinema, 45 prohibit tobacco advertisements in the press, 34 have banned product sampling, 21 countries do not permit point-of-sale advertising, and just 13 have banned tobacco industry sponsorship (of sporting and other events).[38] To date, the US has only put a stop to television and radio advertisements for tobacco.[39]

In 1995, the US Food and Drug Administration (FDA) and President Clinton announced proposed rules to regulate the tobacco industry. In August 1996, the regulations were approved, including advertising and promotion restrictions. These restrictions are a step in the right direction toward ending tobacco marketing to kids. They would limit the use of images and themes that appeal to children, as well as the placement of ads in media widely accessible to youth. The FDA rules even address event sponsorship and "brand stretching," but with significant loopholes. The FDA rules permit sponsorship by tobacco corporations of entertainment and sporting events under corporate names, a loophole that has been exploited in other countries. Indirect advertising is also not sufficiently addressed in the US FDA regulations. While prohibiting the sale and distribution of non-tobacco items that carry cigarette logos, the FDA initiative would also let "corporate" images slip through. However, the advertising and promotion restrictions are significant in that billboard and media advertising would be limited to black and white text only.[40] The US tobacco corporations have held up the regulations by suing the agency to block the advertising and promotion restrictions.

TABLE V
Countries With Partial or Total Tobacco Advertising and Promotion Bans—1997

Country	TV	Radio	Press	Cinema	Sponsorship	Point of Sale	Sampling
Australia	X	X	X	X	Restrictions	Restrictions	Restrictions
Azerbaijan	X	X	X	X		X	X
Bulgaria	X	X	X	X			Restrictions
Canada	X	X	Restrictions	X	Restrictions	X	X
Croatia	X	X	X	X	Restrictions		
Cuba	X	X	X	X	N/A	X	N/A
Czech Rep.	X	X	X	X		Restrictions	Restrictions
Finland	X	X	X	X	X	X	X
France	X	X	X	X	X	Restrictions	X
Iceland	X	X	X	X	Restrictions	X	X
India	X	X	Ban Pending	Ban Pending	Ban Pending	Ban Pending	Ban Pending
Malaysia	X	X	X	X	Restrictions		X
Maldives Isl.	X	X	X	X	X	X	X
Mongolia	X	X	X	X	X	N/A	N/A
New Zealand	X	X	X	X	Restrictions	Restrictions	X
Norway	X	X	X	X	X	Restrictions	X
Portugal	X	X	X	X	Restrictions	Restrictions	
Singapore	X	X	X	X	Restrictions	X	X
Somalia	X	X	X	X	Restrictions		
Sudan	X	X	X	X	N/A	X	N/A
Sweden	X	X	X	X	X	Restrictions	Restrictions
Thailand	X	X	X	X	X	X	X
Vietnam	X	X	X	X	X	Restrictions	

Source: *Smoking Issues Status Book: Global Overview June 1997*, International Tobacco Documentation Center.

In anticipation of new advertising and promotion regulations in the US, Philip Morris and RJR Nabisco have introduced some new tactics already. Philip Morris came out with *Marlboro Unlimited* magazine in 1996, which is mailed directly to some 2 million people,[41] launching the *Virginia Slims* catalog and "Woman Thing Music" label.[42] RJR Nabisco and Philip Morris are beginning to wean the US public off brand names like Marlboro and Winston with billboard ads that either use partial names like "Marl" or "Wins" or omit the names altogether. In addition, ads are being tested with cigarettes that mimic human behavior, in anticipation of legislation that will prohibit the use of people or cartoons in advertising.

Philip Morris launched the *Marlboro Unlimited* magazine targeting young men in 1996. The magazine is part of a direct mail campaign to build on the already enormous database amassed by the corporation in anticipation of US Food and Drug Administration regulations.[43]

Joe Camel Lives On . . .

RJR Nabisco pulled Joe Camel ads in the US in 1997 thanks to public pressure and action taken by the US Federal Trade Commission. However, Joe Camel is now being used to capture the youth market in other regions of the world. Now the US tobacco giants are targeting Africa, fighting for market share in countries like South Africa and Nigeria, the most heavily populated African country with 100 million people.[44]

In 1996, the cartoon advertisement was introduced in Argentina, along with prizes for playing cards inside cigarette packages with the image of Joe Camel. Among the prizes were ten Harley-Davidson motorcycles, which were on display in shopping malls. Camel sales increased by 50 percent in Argentina after the Joe Camel campaign was introduced there.[45]

Event Sponsorship

A recent study by a marketing firm shows that the tobacco transnationals have turned increasingly to sponsoring sporting and other events like auto racing as more countries are passing restrictions on traditional forms of such advertising as billboards, TV, and radio. "The inability to legally advertise their brands directly has led the major tobacco manufacturers to look increasingly towards indirect, or subliminal, advertising to promote their products," according to the marketing research firm Euromonitor International.[46] Indirect advertising must be addressed for local, national, or international laws on tobacco control to be effective.

Event and sports sponsorship is a common loophole the tobacco corporations exploit in countries with direct advertising bans. This Marlboro poster with the widely recognized Marlboro cowboy logo promotes a "Hollywood Nite" event in Vietnam. Photo by Debra Efroymson, PATH Canada, 1997.

In Finland, where there is a ban on any form of direct or indirect tobacco advertising, brand stretching is seen through Marlboro Classics clothes, Camel boots and socks, Camel Trophy matches, and Formula One racing, where Finnish drivers sport uniforms emblazoned with the Marlboro logo, minus the word "Marlboro."[47]

Philip Morris cannot legally use the word "Marlboro" in countries like Finland and Vietnam where direct advertising is banned, but it can get away with the familiar bright red and white wedge logo[48] spotted on these mopeds and inside a store in Vietnam. Photos by Debra Efroymson, PATH Canada, 1997.

In Singapore, Philip Morris provides arts scholarships, and even though cigarette brand names are not permitted for sport and event sponsorship, the tobacco corporations have only to seek permission of the Minister of Health to sponsor competitions, events, and performances in the corporate name. The tobacco corporations are allowed to sell products carrying their brands, like Camel sportswear.[49]

The trade journal *Tobacco International* reported that Hong Kong's ban on cigarette advertising, which passed in 1997 just before the colony reverted to China, is being appealed. US tobacco corporations are looking for any means possible to continue promoting their tobacco products through non-tobacco items, such as Marlboro Classics clothing, and sponsorship of events.[50] Examples of events sponsored by the US tobacco giants in 1996 in China include the Salem Open (tennis) in Hong Kong, the Virginia Slims "My Journey" fashion design auditions in Hong Kong, and the Marlboro Cup (soccer) in Hong Kong. Philip Morris has spent 11 million yuan a year to sponsor the China Football Association (soccer) for the past five years (15 million yuan in 1996).[51] Tobacco control activists in Hong Kong succeeded in getting new advertising regulations put in place to restrict tobacco sponsorship. As a result, Philip Morris withdrew its sponsorship of tennis in Hong Kong in early 1998 because they would not be allowed to use the event to advertise on TV or radio.[52]

R.J. Reynolds convinced the Mongolia Minister of Trade and Tourism to allow advertising for "Camel Trophy '97," a jeep "adventure tour," in spite of a comprehensive tobacco control law passed in 1994 that bans direct and indirect advertising, including sponsorship. R.J. Reynolds even changed the timing of the campaign to coincide with World No Tobacco Day on May 31.[53]

In the UK, there are voluntary limits that prohibit the use of tobacco brand names on race cars. The tobacco corporations simply use the widely recognized logos, like Marlboro's red and white chevron, to get around the rules. Philip Morris has spent $77 million on Formula One racing sponsorships and prizes, more than any other corporation, according to the *New York Times*. Legislation proposed in the US contains similar loopholes on sports sponsorship bans that the tobacco giants are certain to exploit.[54]

Giveaways and Product Sampling

In Vietnam, even though there is a ban on all forms of direct advertising except point of sale (which is restricted), young women dressed in Marlboro outfits can be found distributing cigarettes because product sampling is still permitted.[55]

Young women in Vietnam dressed in Marlboro outfits distribute cigarettes for Philip Morris. Photo by Debra Efroymson, PATH Canada, 1997.

Philip Morris offers Marlboro sportswear in exchange for empty Marlboro cigarette packs in department stores in Beijing, just as China has taken steps to restrict tobacco advertising.[56]

"Brand Stretching"

Philip Morris and RJR Nabisco have proven extremely creative in exploiting any loopholes in laws restricting tobacco advertising and promotion in other countries by using brand logos on clothing or vans, and sponsoring rock concerts. The tactic known as "brand stretching" is used to build tobacco brand-name recognition by promoting the name and/or logo on non-tobacco products.

Vans covered with tobacco logos are like moving billboards. A Camel van in Senegal, 1996. Photo by Anna White. A Marlboro van in Vietnam, 1997. Photo by Debra Efroymson, PATH Canada.

Worldwide Brands Inc., a subsidiary of RJR Nabisco Holdings, has the licensing rights to RJR Nabisco's tobacco trademarks for other products. Camel Boots, for example, is not owned directly by RJR Nabisco but by another company that acquired the rights to use the name Camel through an agreement with WBI, incorporated by RJR Nabisco in Switzerland.[57] Worldwide Brands executives claim to be only in the apparel business. In South Africa, Worldwide Brands runs the Camel Trophy event, in addition to holding the trademark for Camel Trophy Brands, including boots, watches, clothing, and bags.[58]

RJR Nabisco's Worldwide Brands helps the tobacco corporation avoid direct ad bans by licensing out tobacco trademarks for non-tobacco items like Camel boots, watches, and clothing—a practice known as "brand stretching."[59]

Salem Holidays Sdn. Bhd. and Salem Power Station Sdn. Bhd. are both incorporated in Malaysia and are listed as subsidiaries of RJR Nabisco Holdings. Camel Racing Inc. is incorporated in Canada.[60] Marlboro Classics (the clothing label) has been marketed in China by Vigor International (HK) Ltd., and the products are sold in retail outlets in Beijing, Guangzhou, and Shanghai.[61] Marlboro Classics does not appear to have been incorporated, although there are some 1,000 Marlboro Classics stores in Europe and Asia.[62] A subsidiary called Philip Morris Products incorporated in the US may have a similar licensing purpose to that of RJR Nabisco's Worldwide Brands.[63]

In addition, Singapore and Thailand receive television broadcasts from Malaysia, where indirect advertising for tobacco products is rampant in spite of the direct advertising ban. RJR Nabisco advertises Salem Attitude clothing with the same logo and colors as Salem cigarettes. Marlboro Classics clothing, Salem Power Station Music stores, and B.A.T's Benson & Hedges Bistro are also widely advertised.[64]

'93 FALL & WINTER COLLECTION

Salem ATTITUDE

LANDMARK SHOP : 83 Basement One Gloucester One Central 523 6212 • LANE CRAWFORD • CITYPLAZA SHOP 268 Cityplaza II Taikoo Shing 569 3638

This 1993 ad for RJR Nabisco's Salem Attitude clothing in a Hong Kong magazine is a form of "brand stretching"— using tobacco names, logos, or colors on non-tobacco items. The ads are widely used in Asia, including Malaysia and Hong Kong where there are bans on direct tobacco advertising.[65]

Internal documents from R.J. Reynolds International in Geneva prepared for advertising agency McCann-Erickson in Hong Kong state that "'Salem Attitude' is established to extend the trademark beyond tobacco category restrictions."[66]

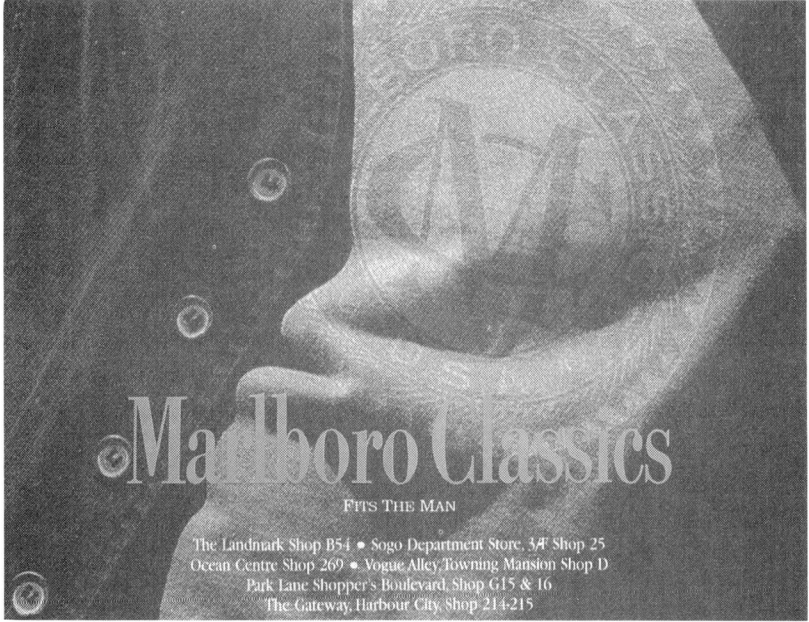

A Philip Morris ad for Marlboro Classics clothing from a Hong Kong paper. Marlboro Classics stores are widely advertised. Countries that have Marlboro Classics clothing stores include China (Hong Kong), Belgium, Denmark, France, Germany, Greece, Holland, Indonesia, Italy, Japan, Korea, Norway, Portugal, Sweden, Taiwan, Thailand, and the UK.[67]

In 1993, Tabacalera, Spain's state-run tobacco company, joined with RJR Nabisco in a joint venture called RJR Alimentacion [Nutrition] SL which owns Royal Brands. The joint venture was formed to "produce, distribute and market" Camel and Winston brands for RJR Nabisco.[68] In Spain, Winston sponsors rock concerts, and cigarette brands and logos are used on non-tobacco products and travel services.[69]

Brand stretching by RJR Nabisco and other tobacco transnationals is rampant in South Africa, with Camel clothing, the Camel Hour (music for young people), and Camel Party Zone CDs from Camel music productions.[70] Similarly, in Thailand, which has a complete ad ban, there are Marlboro Classics stores and Camel Trophy clothing, and Philip Morris sponsors Asian arts awards.[71]

RJR Nabisco opened the first US cigarette manufacturing fa-

cility in Poland in 1994.[72] Poland, which is in a region with the
highest death rates in the world from tobacco,[73] passed legislation
in 1996 banning sales of cigarettes in vending machines and sports
arenas, prohibiting TV and radio ads, as well as ads in newspapers
and magazines for youth, and the cinema.[74] Yet, children and youth
are targeted with posters for Camel Planet next to schools,[75] promotions in discos, restaurants, even a circus-tent event with free
cigarettes at the beach.[76]

A 1996 ad for Camel Planet, a nightclub promotion in Poland. The message in the ad taken from a Polish car magazine is "Remember! Camel
Planet. The Earth is ours. You have no alternative. Either you come to us
or we come to you." Posters like this can be seen just outside schools in
Poland.[77]

Many of the former communist regimes of Eastern Europe and the Soviet Republics prohibited tobacco advertising. After the fall of communism, the tobacco transnationals launched major ad campaigns. Hungary had such a ban, which was ignored in the post-communist era. Philip Morris, RJR Nabisco, and B.A.T formed a manufacturers association to lobby for a voluntary marketing code in lieu of the advertising restrictions. Advertising over the past decade has increased dramatically as a result. In response to the barrage of tobacco advertising, Hungarian officials began to enforce laws from the communist era, but the tobacco transnationals openly defied the laws. The Hungarian parliament passed new tobacco advertising restrictions in June 1997; these have already been reversed in a victory for the tobacco industry.[78]

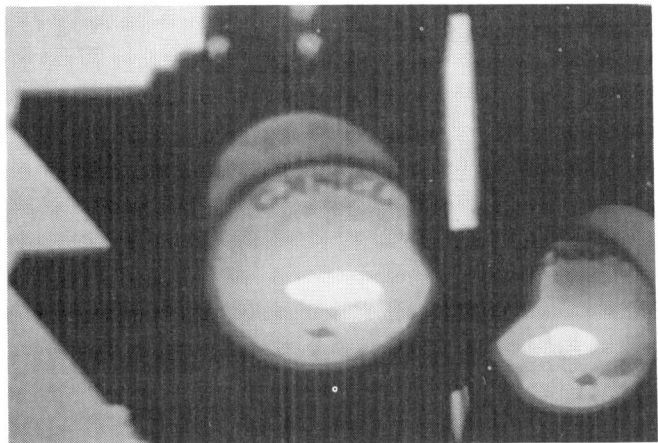

RJR Nabisco's Camel logo is emblazoned on everything from stoplights to trolley cars in Romania.[79]

In the Czech Republic, RJR Nabisco has even promoted "Camel" weddings with taxis emblazoned with the brand logo.[80]

In Australia, where the only advertising permitted is point-of-sale (in some states) and certain international sporting events (including Formula One Grand Prix), the tobacco corporations have exploited a loophole in the legislation to sell packets of cigarettes with giveaways, such as key rings, stubby coolers, music and video tapes, hats, diaries, etc. None of the items can have tobacco brand names on them, but they often use the same coloring as the cigarette packs. This practice has been stopped in some states, but continues in others.[81]

Violating the Law

Thailand has a total ban on tobacco advertising, some of the strictest laws in the world, yet enforcement is weak when the laws are violated.[82]

When China hosted the 10th World Conference on Tobacco or Health in August 1997, few ads were visible for Camel or Marlboro since an ad ban in ten cities, including Beijing, had just gone into effect.[83] Umbrellas with brand names like Camel had been painted over, or removed from site. However, trinkets from outside Beijing could be found—like Marlboro tissue packs which look like cigarette packs. When the Conference ended, advertising for Marlboro and Camel reappeared in Beijing, in violation of the ad ban. Marlboro ads and cigarettes often appeared alongside Philip Morris's Kraft ads and products.[84]

In South Africa, the 1993 law regarding the placement of mandatory health warnings and tar/nicotine content is routinely ignored.[85] South Africa threatened to ban all tobacco advertising in 1996 unless the warning laws were respected.[86]

In Bulgaria, in spite of the TV ad ban, television ads are still shown for Marlboro, they just don't show cigarettes. National companies have not traditionally advertised, but are starting to in order to compete with

Marlboro key chains from Thailand violate the country's total ban on advertising. Courtesy of Bung On Ritthiphakdee, ASH Thailand, 1997.

In China, Marlboro tissue packs were found after a direct advertising ban was passed in 1997. Camel umbrellas in Beijing were painted over during the 10th World Conference on Tobacco or Health held in the city in August 1997.

Philip Morris and RJR Nabisco. Concerts are tobacco-sponsored, and the tobacco corporations give out free samples. The only restriction is that pictures of actual cigarettes cannot be shown, so the corporations simply black out where cigarettes used to be in the ads.[87]

Undermining Health Warnings

Some of the most shrewd ads can be seen in the UK, where the tobacco corporations parody British health warnings, and use death imagery as another advertising tool.[88] In Brazil, the tobacco corporations also parody health warnings in their advertisements, and use phrases like "Isso é legal," which in Portuguese has two meanings: "This is the law" and "this is cool." The tobacco corporations have introduced youth "anti-smoking" programs in coordination with the Brazilian government through an industry association called ABIFUMO. Philip Morris is represented by ABIFUMO in Brazil. The program uses slogans like "Smoking is an adult decision."[89]

Philip Morris has introduced youth anti-smoking programs in several countries, including Brazil, where smoking is promoted as an adult decision.
Similar programs in the US were found to be ineffective. In Brazil, the
message "Isso é legal" has two meanings: "This is the law" and "This is
cool."[90]

Philip Morris's Action Against Access program in the US uses
similar slogans, and was found generally ineffective even by independent evaluator Warren Rudman—who was hand-picked by Philip
Morris.[91] Internal documents from the Tobacco Institute, the lobbying arm for the tobacco industry in the US, revealed a more sin-
ister side to its youth "anti-smoking" program, which was in fact
designed to have the opposite effect[92] by associating smoking as
an "adult" activity. Now similar programs are being used internationally.[93]

Internal Industry Documents Reveal Tobacco Advertising and Promotion Schemes

A regional manager of RJR Nabisco in Eastern Europe commented to the press, "Our interest is not to increase the per capita
smoking but to have the people who are already smoking to smoke
more of our brands."[94]

Yet internal documents from both RJR Nabisco and Philip
Morris demonstrate that the corporations will not voluntarily limit

their advertising and promotion of tobacco to adults. A 1990 memo from RJR instructs its sales force to identify stores in close proximity to high schools.[95] **Another internal document from R.J. Reynolds Tobacco Company states the corporation "has a great opportunity to capitalize on the growing foreign market, particularly the market in 'emerging nations.'"** This same document also says, "Evidence is now available to indicate that the 14- to-18-year-old group is an increasing segment of the smoking population. RJR *must soon* establish a successful *new* brand in this market if our position in the industry is to be maintained over the long term"[96] (emphasis in the original). And in 1988, along came Joe Camel.[97]

Philip Morris and RJR Nabisco have proven very creative in circumventing existing advertising restrictions around the world by exploiting loopholes in the law, and in some cases simply ignoring the law. This abusive behavior serves as an important lesson for countries seeking to restrict or ban tobacco marketing and promotion. The tobacco corporations exploit every opportunity to advertise and promote their product. Such behavior makes a strong case that supranational standards governing tobacco advertising and promotion would strengthen national efforts to control this public health menace.

NOTES

1   "Top Global Marketers," *Advertising Age International*, Nov. 1997, p. 9.

2   "Global Media & Marketing," *Advertising Age International*, Dec. 14, 1992, p. s-1, and "Top Global Marketers," *Advertising Age International*, Nov. 1997, p. 9.

3   *Advertising Age International*, July 1997, pp. i25-i27.

4   Personal communication with Craig Endicott, *Advertising Age International*, Oct. 1, 1997 and March 9, 1998.

5   Anna White, "Joe Camel's World Tour," (op-ed), *New York Times*, April 23, 1997.

6   A 1997 Philip Morris ad provided by Eva Kralikova, MD, Charles University, Czech Republic.

7   Richard W. Stevenson, "Tapping a Rich Smoking Frontier," *New*

York Times, Nov. 12, 1993.

8   Alexander V. Prokhorov, "Getting on Smokin' Route 66: To-bacco Promotion via Russian Mass Media," *Tobacco Control*, Summer 1997, vol. 6, pp. 145-146.

9   A 1997 ad provided by Eva Kralikova, MD, Charles University, Czech Republic.

10   "Top 10 Marketers in 56 Countries," *Advertising Age International*, Nov. 1997, p. 10; *Smoking Issues Status Book: Global Overview June 1997*, International Tobacco Documentation Center.

11   "Top 10 Marketers in 56 Countries," *Advertising Age International*, Nov. 1997, p. 10; Dr. Zarihah M. Zain, Ministry of Health (Malaysia) and Mary Assunta (Consumers Association of Penang), "Circumvention of Bans on Direct Advertising," (paper presented at the 10th World Conference on Tobacco or Health), Beijing, Aug. 1997, p. 4.

12   Dr. Zarihah M. Zain, Ministry of Health (Malaysia) and Mary Assunta (Consumers Association of Penang), "Circumvention of Bans on Direct Advertising," (paper presented at the 10th World Conference on Tobacco or Health), Beijing, Aug. 1997, p. 1.

13   "Cigarette Advertising Code," The Tobacco Institute, p. 7; "Cigarette Advertising and Promotion Code," The Tobacco Institute, Dec. 1990.

14   Glenn John, *Tobacco International*, Aug. 1996, p. 3.

15   Produced in 1993, the Summer Party CD was the top-selling CD that year. Provided by Grover Ho, Hong Kong.

16   Photo of Primary School No. 1 is less than 300 feet from the Camel Planet club on the same street. Nicholas Copernicus High School in Torun is next to the Camel kiosk. Health Promotion Foundation and Center for Cancer Epidemiology and Prevention, and teacher at Nicholas Copernicus University, Poland, Oct. 1996.

17   R.J. Reynolds ad in *The Onion* (weekly alternative), March 12-18, 1997, p. 24.

18   Philip Morris US brochure/catalog copyrighted 1998. The Camel brochure is from 1997, by R.J. Reynolds and advertis-

ing agency McCann-Erickson, and provided by Eva Kralikova, MD, Charles University, Czech Republic.

19 Photo taken by Susan Ritter, Oxfam, 1994, in Cambodia.

20 Testimony of Philip Morris CEO Geoffrey Bible, US House Commerce Committee, Jan. 29, 1998. Photo courtesy of Susan Ritter, Oxfam, 1994.

21 Photos taken by INFACT during 10th World Conference on Tobacco or Health, Beijing, Aug. 27, 1997.

22 Photo taken in Kenya, 1988, and provided courtesy of Dr. Greg Connolly, Massachusetts Department of Public Health, Boston, MA.

23 Testimony by the CEOs of Philip Morris, RJR Nabisco, et.al., witnessed at the January 29, 1998 hearings before the US House Commerce Committee

24 Testimony by the CEOs of Philip Morris, RJR Nabisco, et.al., witnessed at the January 29, 1998 hearings before the US House Commerce Committee.

25 Personal communication with Nobuko Nakano, Women's Action on Smoking, Tokyo, Feb. 10, 1998; "Outline of Voluntary Rules," Tobacco Institute of Japan, established April 1985, modified Oct. 1995.

26 Ira Teinowitz and Christy Fisher, "Philip Morris' $10B Warning," *Advertising Age International,* March 28, 1994, p. 2.

27 Philip Morris 1996 and 1997 lobbying reports, Legislative Resource Center.

28 Telephone communication, US Food and Drug Administration, Nov. 1997.

29 Ann Potempa, "Cigarette Maker's Letter Asks Oscar Employees for Support," *Capital Times,* Dec. 1, 1995.

30 "Tobacco Firm Donates Heavily to Convention," (AP) *Baltimore Sun,* Aug. 25, 1996.

31 *Advertising Age International* (chart), Sept. 1997, pp. i11, i24.

32 *Advertising Age International*, April 15, 1996, p. s15.

33 Barry Meier, "Tobacco Industry, Conciliatory in U.S., Goes on the Attack in the Third World," *New York Times*, Jan. 18, 1998.

34 Mike France, William Symonds, Monica Larner, Dave Lindorff, "The World War on Tobacco," *Business Week*, Nov. 11, 1996, p. 99.

35 "An International Framework Convention for Tobacco Control," Neil E. Collishaw of the World Health Organization (Presentation at the 10th World Conference on Tobacco or Health), Beijing, Aug., 1997; personal communication with Dr. Judith Mackay, Asian Consultancy on Tobacco Control, March 4, 1998.

36 World Health Organization Fact Sheet #118, "The Tobacco Epidemic: A Global Public Health Emergency," May 1996, p. 5.

37 Nancy Stancill, "Teen-age Smoking Explodes Globally," *Charlotte Observer*, Oct. 20, 1997.

38 *Smoking Issues Status Book: Global Overview*, International Tobacco Documentation Centre, June 1997, p. 3.

39 Federal Trade Commission Report to Congress for 1994, Issued: 1996, p. 14.

40 The US Food and Drug Administration, "The Regulations Restricting the Sale and Distribution of Cigarettes and Smokeless Tobacco to Protect Children and Adolescents" (Executive Summary-internet version), Aug. 1996.

41 Sally Goll Beatty, "Philip Morris Starts Lifestyle Magazine," *Wall Street Journal*, Sept. 16, 1996.

42 Patrick M. Reilly, "Virginia Slims Gets Its Own Record Label," *Wall Street Journal*, Jan. 15, 1997.

43 Premier issue of *Marlboro Unlimited*. Copyrighted by Philip Morris, 1996.

44 Matthew Bunce, "Joe Camel Steps Into Africa," *Sunday Argus* (Cape Town), Aug. 10, 1997.

45 ASH (London) Daily News Round-up, Sept. 11, 1996.

46 Nancy Stancill, "Teen-age Smoking Explodes Globally," *Charlotte Observer*, Oct. 20, 1997.

47 Mervi Hara, Finland ASH, response to INFACT survey, Aug. 6, 1997.

48 Mervi Hara, Finland ASH, response to INFACT survey, Aug. 6, 1997; *Smoking Issues Status Book: Global Overview June*

1997, International Tobacco Documentation Center.

49 Personal communication with Chng Chee Yeong, Ministry of Health (Singapore), 10th World Conference on Tobacco or Health, Beijing, Aug. 1997; "National Smoking Control Programme: The Singapore Experience," 1986-1996, Chng Chee Yeong, Ministry of Health (Singapore).

50 "New Bid To Save $780M in Billings," *Tobacco International*, Aug. 1997, p. 29.

51 Personal communication with Dr. Judith Mackay, Asian Consultancy on Tobacco Control, Dec. 10, 1997.

52 "Tobacco Giant Pulls Out of HK Tennis Sponsorship," Reuters, Feb. 10, 1998 (from SCARCNet).

53 Personal communication with Dr. Judith Mackay, Asian Consultancy on Tobacco Control, May 17, 1997.

54 Barry Meier, "A Controversy on Tobacco Road," *New York Times*, Dec. 4, 1997.

55 *Smoking Issues Status Book: Global Overview June 1997*, International Tobacco Documentation Center.

56 "Philip Morris Offers Sportswear for Packs," *Advertising Age International*, Jan. 1998, p. 2.

57 Personal communication with Paul Nordgren, Swedish Institute of Public Health, Feb. 11, 1998; *Who Owns Whom: North America* (United Kingdom: Dun & Bradstreet, 1997), pp. 202-203; letter from Grant Henderson, Market Co-ordinator, Camel Trophy South Africa, to Ken Sheppard, Tobacco Action Committee, South Africa, May 1997.

58 Letter from Grant Henderson, Market Co-ordinator, Camel Trophy South Africa, to Ken Sheppard, Tobacco Action Committee, South Africa, May 1997.

59 Ad from *Cosmopolitan,* May 1997. Copyright R.J. Reynolds, 1997.

60 *Who Owns Whom.* (United Kingdom: Dun & Bradstreet, 1997), pp. 202-203.

61 "China Gets Casual with Marlboro Classics," *China Avenue Magazine*, March-May 1996, p. 36; Personal communication with Dr. Judith Mackay, Asian Consultancy on Tobacco Con-

trol, Jan. 19, 1997.

62   Fara Warner, "Tobacco Brands Outmaneuver Asian Ad Bans,"
     Wall Street Journal, Aug. 6, 1996.

63   *Who Owns Whom: North America.* (United Kingdom: Dun &
     Bradstreet Ltd., 1997), p. 175; personal communication with
     Paul Nordgren, Swedish Institute of Public Health, Feb. 11,
     1998.

64   Presentation by Dr. Zarihah Mohd Zain of Malaysia, 10th World
     Conference on Tobacco or Health, Beijing, Aug. 1997.

65   Ad provided by Grover Ho, Hong Kong. Copyright by RJR
     Nabisco.

66   Fara Warner, "Tobacco Brands Outmaneuver Asian Ad Bans,"
     Wall Street Journal, Aug. 6, 1996.

67   Advertisements for Marlboro Classics appeared in the *Sunday
     Morning Post Magazine* (Hong Kong), March 19, 1995 and
     China Avenue Magazine, March-May 1996, p. 36; personal com-
     munication with Dr. Judith Mackay, Asian Consultancy on To-
     bacco Control, Feb. 16, 1997; INFACT survey completed by
     Bung On Ritthiphakdee, ASH Thailand, July 25, 1997. Ad pro-
     vided by Grover Ho, Hong Kong. Copyright by Philip Morris,
     1995.

68   "Tabacalera SA," *Wall Street Journal*, June 21, 1993.

69   Presentation by Dr. José Calvo of Spain, 10th World Confer-
     ence on Tobacco or Health, Beijing, Aug. 1997.

70   Personal communication with Ken Sheppard, Tobacco Action
     Committee, South Africa, Feb. 6, 1997 and Feb. 12, 1998.

71   INFACT survey completed by Bung On Ritthiphakdee, ASH
     Thailand, July 25, 1997.

72   "RJR New Markets: A Thirst for Being First," *Tobacco Inter-
     national*, March 1995, p. 34.

73   Lawrence Holland, "The East: Marlboro Man Rides High As
     Smoking, Death Rates Soar," Radio Free Europe/Radio Lib-
     erty, June 26, 1997 (internet version).

74   "Tobacco or Health: A Global Status Report," World Health
     Organization Tobacco or Health Programme, 1997; Mike
     France, William Symonds, Monica Larner, Dave Lindorff, "The

World War on Tobacco," *Business Week*, Nov. 11, 1996, p. 99.

75 Personal communication with Scott Thompson, Health Promotion Foundation and Center for Cancer Epidemiology and Prevention of Poland, Dec. 3, 1996.

76 Nancy Stancill, "Teen-age Smoking Explodes Globally," *Charlotte Observer*, Oct. 20, 1997.

77 Ad taken from a Polish magazine, *Auto*, No. 9 (70), wrzesien 1996; personal communication with Scott Thompson, Health Promotion Foundation and Center for Cancer Epidemiology and Prevention of Poland, and teacher, Nicholas Copernicus High School, Dec. 3, 1996.

78 William Beaver, "The Marlboro Man Rides Into the Eastern Bloc," *Business and Society Review*, January 1994, p. 21; Ken Kasreil, "Western Tobacco Firms Spurn Hungary's Ad Ban," *Advertising Age International*, Sept. 14, 1992, p. 60 (SCARCNet Summary); "Against Tide, Parliament Eases Ad Regulations," *Tobacco International*, Sept. 1997, p. 75.

79 Photos courtesy of Dr. Greg Connelly, Massachusetts Department of Public Health, and Toxicomanies Cooperation, France. The stoplight photo was taken in Romania in Aug. 1993.

80 Myron Levin, "Targeting Foreign Smokers," *Los Angeles Times*, Nov. 17, 1994.

81 Jane Martin, Information and Policy Manager, Quit Victoria (Australia), response to INFACT survey, July 31, 1997; personal communication with Jane Martin, Quit Victoria, Feb. 12, 1998.

82 Presentation by Prakit Vatheesatokit, ASH Thailand, at the 10th World Conference on Tobacco or Health, Beijing, Aug. 25, 1997.

83 Zhu Baoxia, "Conference to Support Anti-Smoking Struggle," *China Daily,* Aug. 22, 1997.

84 Personal observation by INFACT representatives at 10th World Conference on Tobacco or Health, Beijing, Aug. 1997.

85 Personal communication with Ken Sheppard, Tobacco Action Committee, South Africa, Oct. 23, 1997.

86 Matthew Bunce, "Joe Camel Steps Into Africa," *Sunday Argus*

(Cape Town), Aug. 10, 1997.

87 Personal communication with Dr. George Katarov of Bulgaria, 10th World Conference on Tobacco or Health, Beijing, Aug. 1997.

88 Laurel Wentz, "Tobacco Marketers Eye Global Models for U.S.," *Advertising Age International*, May 12, 1997, p. 22.

89 Laurel Wentz, "Tobacco Marketers Eye Global Models for U.S.," *Advertising Age International*, May 12, 1997, p. 22; personal communication with Dr. Luiza Costa e Silva Goldfarb, National Institute of Cancer, Brazil, Aug. 18, 1997; letter from Philip Morris Brasil to the president of the National Institute of Cancer, Brazil, July 28, 1997.

90 1997 poster courtesy of Dr. Luiza Costa e Silva Goldfarb, National Institute of Cancer, Brazil.

91 Doug Levy, "Tobacco Plan Has Some Success," *USA Today*, June 2, 1997, p. D1 (SCARCNet Summary).

92 Milo Geyelin, "Official in Florida Finds Evidence on Tobacco Group Teen Program," *Wall Street Journal*, Aug. 6, 1997.

93 Personal communication with Dr. Luiza Costa e Silva Goldfarb, National Institute of Cancer, Brazil, Aug. 18, 1997; personal communication with Eva Kralikova, MD, Charles University, Czech Republic, Sept. 9, 1997; personal communication with Philip Morris CEO Geoffrey Bible, Washington, DC, Jan. 29, 1998. Mr. Bible said they have introduced programs in 37 countries.

94 Jane Perlez, "R.J. Reynolds Woos Polish Smokers," *New York Times*, June 6, 1994.

95 Letter from J.P. McMahon of RJR Sales Company in Sarasota, Florida to sales representatives, January 10, 1990.

96 R.J. Reynolds Tobacco Company internal document, "Planning Assumptions and Forecast for the Period 1976-1986 for R.J. Reynolds Tobacco Company," Research Department, March 15, 1976, p. 4, and section "E. Products" (emphasis in the original).

97 Stuart Elliott, "Joe Camel, A Giant in Tobacco Marketing, Is Dead at 23," *New York Times*, July 11, 1997.

INFLUENCE-PEDDLING OF PHILIP MORRIS AND RJR NABISCO

The US-based tobacco transnationals are able to get around advertising and promotion regulations because of their heavy involvement in the development of, and their enormous influence over the outcome of, public policy. Through this influence, these corporations safeguard their access to new young customers. Political contributions, lobbying, front groups, advocacy advertising, and creating the appearance of grassroots support ("astroturf" lobbying) are some of the tactics Philip Morris and RJR Nabisco have used to ensure their position of strength in US policymaking.[1]

In the US, Philip Morris was the #1 political contributor during the 1995-96 election cycle—the most expensive elections in US history—with contributions of $4.2 million.[2] In addition, in 1997 the tobacco corporations spent at least $30 million lobbying to influence policy protecting their interests. That figure is expected to increase in 1998.[3] It is this political stronghold in the US that provides the corporations with political muster at the international level as well. Former Texas governor Ann Richards, and former Senate Majority Leader George Mitchell are just two of the very influential people now on the payroll of the US tobacco industry. Former presidential candidate and US Senate Majority Leader Bob Dole also works for tobacco lobbying firm Verner, Liipfert, Bernhard, McPherson & Hand.[4]

To gain access to new markets, Philip Morris and RJR Nabisco have hired very high-profile political consultants with enormous influence. Philip Morris hired former British prime minister Margaret Thatcher at £500,000 per year (about US$ 815,000) to use her clout to break into markets in central Europe, the former Soviet republics, China and Vietnam.[5]

Philip Morris uses front groups like the New York Society for International Affairs, the America-European Community Association, and Libertad Inc. to arrange trips for elected officials to Africa, Australia, Europe, and elsewhere. All three groups are alleged to have been founded by, or have a board connection with, Andrew Whist, a Philip Morris senior vice president, and to have been substantially or even solely funded by Philip Morris.[6]

When the European Commission introduced the idea of expanding an ad ban from television to all forms of media distributed in more than one member state, Philip Morris responded with an advertising blitz in national newspapers across Europe with the message that such legislation restricts the "personal liberty" of smokers.[7] The advertising campaign was similar to the campaigns by Philip Morris and RJR Nabisco in the US in 1995 in response to the proposed FDA regulations.[8] The European Union ad ban did pass in late 1997, but many of the advertising and promotion restrictions will not take effect for several years.[9] The tobacco corporations have already identified loopholes in the new law:

> [A]lthough use of symbols and trade marks to get around the ban on tobacco advertising will be outlawed, firms may continue to show advertising using a trademark associated with both a tobacco product and another type of product—such as jeans or footwear—provided the non-tobacco product has been on the market for some time ahead of the adoption of the directive and that it accounts for more than double the tobacco turnover.[10]

The US-based tobacco corporations are big campaign contributors in international elections, which has apparently proved as effective overseas as in the US. British Prime Minister Tony Blair made promises during his campaign to crack down on tobacco advertising and promotion, but has come under fire for exempting Formula One racing from the ban on tobacco sports sponsorship. Philip Morris is the #1 advertiser for Formula One, and Blair's Labour Party received a $1.7-million campaign contribution from the head of the racing organization.[11] A tobacco trade publication reported that the "beneficials" to the Labour Party "left the Labour health minister pledging for an exemption of sport sponsoring from the overall tobacco ban."[12] The prime minister has since returned £100,000 to the Formula One chief as a result of the controversy.[13]

Philip Morris and RJR Nabisco have also courted favor with international media. In 1997, Philip Morris flew Russian journalists from Moscow to a dinner party complete with caviar, liquor, salmon, and cigarettes, at one of the corporation's factories in Krasnodar. A Russian PR person was on the scene to hand out free Marlboro shirts, hats, and other paraphernalia.[14] RJR Nabisco sponsored a trip for prominent Czech journalists to Germany in the spring of 1996, which may have been intended to preempt coverage around upcoming issues on tobacco—according to a local tobacco control activist. Philip Morris also organized a trip to Switzerland for members of the Czech parliament in 1994.[15]

The CEO of Philip Morris, Geoffrey Bible, met directly with Chinese President Jiang Zemin in October 1997. President Jiang Zemin expressed his gratitude to the corporation and the CEO in getting the US government to grant China an unconditional (i.e., not tied to human rights) extension of Most Favored Nation status. President Jiang Zemin also said he hoped for new areas of cooperation in the future with Philip Morris, and Bible readily agreed to increase cooperation with Chinese companies.[16] The meeting came less than two months after China hosted the 10th World Conference on Tobacco or Health, where President Jiang Zemin delivered the opening address.

As one of the country's largest investors, Philip Morris also has direct access to Lithuania's prime minister. Philip Morris's Kraft Jacobs Suchard marketing manager commented that the "business climate has changed for the better," after two meetings with prime minister Gediminas Vagnorius.[17] In 1995, Philip Morris drafted a law on manufacturing, growing, and advertising of tobacco later approved by the Lithuanian parliament. Philip Morris also has close ties to the Minister of Agriculture, according to a local tobacco control leader.[18]

Deputy Prime Minister Jiri Skalicky of the Czech Republic, who is also Minister of the Environment, resigned in February 1998 as a result of a secret campaign donation scandal involving Philip Morris and other donors.[19]

The US tobacco corporations' interest in preventing or undermining policies on tobacco control is connected to the success of some of these policies in reducing demand for cigarettes. A tobacco industry trade journal reports that Venezuela's recent drop in cigarette consumption may be a result of new tobacco control legislation. "Venezuela's relatively new anti-smoking policy may also be having an impact on cigarette use. The new smoking policy prohibits smoking on domestic airline flights, in schools, and in certain areas of more exclusive restaurants. In addition, there is a total ban on cigarette advertising on the radio and television."[20]

In most countries and regions where Philip Morris and RJR Nabisco have an interest, the corporations actively lobby to protect that interest. A representative of the Ministry of Health in Thailand said, "They [Philip Morris and RJR Nabisco] try to lobby politicians and obstruct the Ministerial rule about the disclosure of the cigarette ingredients."[21] In Singapore, when cigarette tax increases are proposed, the Tobacco Association, which includes Philip Morris and RJR Nabisco, writes a letter to the Finance Ministry.[22]

The Philip Morris and RJR Nabisco boards of directors include individuals with enormous influence: former government officials, bankers, and media moguls. Recently, Philip Morris added Carlos Slim of Mexico to its board of directors,[23] the richest person in Latin America, with a net worth of some $6.6 billion. He chairs Teléfonos de México (Telmex), is a friend of former President Carlos Salinas, and is a major stockholder in Mexico's largest commercial bank.[24] Other board members with international influence include media tycoon Rupert Murdoch of Philip Morris's board, best known as CEO of News Corporation Limited and owner of FOX television network.[25] Rozanne Ridgway, former Assistant Secretary of State and former US ambassador to Germany, has recently joined RJR Nabisco's board.[26]

NOTES

1   *The 1997 People's Annual Report*, INFACT, pp. 13-17, 20-23.

2   Jill Abramson, " '96 Campaign Costs Set Record at $2.2 Billion," *New York Times*, Nov. 24, 1997.

3   Jill Abramson and Barry Meier, "Tobacco Braced for Costly Fight," *New York Times*, Dec. 15, 1997.

4   Verner, Liipfert, Bernhard, McPherson & Hand home page, Dec. 25, 1997 (www.verner.com); "Richards Hired As Tobacco Lobbyist" (UPI), July 28, 1997 (internet); Jill Abramson and Barry Meier, "Tobacco Braced for Costly Fight," *New York Times*, Dec. 15, 1997.

5   Francis Wheen, "Faggy Thatcher's Trail of Smoke," *Guardian* (England), May 31, 1995, p. 5; Myron Levin, "Targeting Foreign Smokers," *Los Angeles Times*, Nov. 17, 1994.

6   Steve Schultze and Daniel Bice, "Philip Morris Helped Fund Trips," *Journal Sentinel* (Wisconsin), July 30, 1997.

7   "Philip Morris Is Faulted on Ad in Europe," *New York Times*, Nov. 23, 1995.

8   Advertisements were placed in newspapers and magazines by RJR Nabisco and Philip Morris throughout the country. Two examples include "Has the Government Got Its Priorities Right?," an ad by R.J. Reynolds with a photo of "anti-smoking police" arresting a smoker, *Boston Globe*, Oct. 17, 1995, p. 11; and a Philip Morris ad called "Accommodation," *Wall Street Journal*, June 9, 1995.

9   "EU Health Ministers Reach Accord to Ban Most Tobacco Ads," *Wall Street Journal*, Dec. 5, 1997.

10 "Challenges to Proposed E.U. Ad Ban," *Tobacco International*, Dec. 1997, p. 61.

11 Barry Meier, "A Controversy on Tobacco Road," *New York Times*, Dec. 4, 1997.

12 Manfred Korner, "On Fire," *Tobacco International*, Dec. 1997, p. 53.

13 Kevin Maguire, "Blair Returns Pounds 100,000 Gift" (London) *Daily Record*, Nov. 11, 1997, p. 13.

14 Erin Arvedlund, "Earnings After Junkets, Dirges, and Inebriation," *Fortune*, Feb. 17, 1997, p. 32.

15 Personal communication with Eva Kralikova, MD, Charles University, Czech Republic, 10th World Conference on Tobacco or Health, Beijing, Aug. 1997.

16 "Chinese President Meets with Philip Morris Chairman," COMTEX Newswire, Oct. 7, 1997.

17 Latour, Almar, "Lithuania's Remade Economy Draws the Attention of Investors in the West," *Wall Street Journal*, Dec. 1, 1997.

18 INFACT survey completed by Tomas Stanikas, Kaunas Medical Academy, Lithuania, at the 10th World Conference on Tobacco or Health, Beijing, Aug. 1997.

19 "Havel Asks Czech Vice-PM to Postpone Resignation" (Reuters), Central Europe Online, Feb. 18, 1998.

20 "Report from the U.S. Department of Agriculture," *Tobacco International*, Sept. 1997, p. 62.

21 INFACT survey completed by V. Bhumiomanai, Ministry of Public Health, Thailand, at the 10th World Conference on Tobacco or Health, Beijing, Aug. 1997.

22 Personal communication with Chng Chee Yeong, Ministry of Health (Singapore), 10th World Conference on Tobacco or Health, Beijing, Aug. 1997.

23 Philip Morris press release, "Carlos Slim Elected to Board of Directors of Philip Morris Companies Inc.," Aug. 27, 1997.

24 "The Global Power Elite," Kerry A. Dolan (Ed.), *Forbes*, July 28, 1997, p. 99; Carlos Marichal, "The Rapid Rise of the Neobanqueros," NACLA Report on the Americas, May/June 1997, p. 29.

25 Philip Morris 1996 Annual Report, p. 54.

26 RJR Nabisco Annual Report 1996, p. 76.

INTERNATIONAL TARGET MARKETS FOR PHILIP MORRIS AND RJR NABISCO

> The international tobacco business has become an increasingly important source of earnings for RJR Nabisco and can be the most significant driver of our future tobacco earnings growth.—*Steven Goldstone, CEO RJR Nabisco, 1998. ("RJR Restructures Worldwide Tobacco Business,"* Tobacco Reporter, *Feb. 1998, p. 10.)*

Russia, Eastern Europe, the former Soviet Republics, and Asia are key target markets for expansion of the US-based tobacco corporations. The following is an examination of Philip Morris and RJR Nabisco tobacco promotion activities in two target areas—Malaysia and Ukraine—told from the perspective of individuals living and working for consumer protection, public health, and corporate accountability in each of these regions.

Abusive International Marketing and Promotion Tactics by Philip Morris and RJR Nabisco in Ukraine

by Konstantin Krasovsky, Alcohol and
Drug Information Centre, Ukraine

History of the Invasion of the US-based Tobacco Transnationals in Ukraine

A cigarette shortage in cities across the Soviet Union in 1990 opened the door for tobacco transnationals Philip Morris and RJR Nabisco. The US tobacco giants agreed to deliver 34 billion cigarettes, and in return they gained a permanent stronghold in the formerly restricted and potentially lucrative market.[1] US tobacco corporations were some of the first investors to enter Russia and the former Soviet republics, bringing a barrage of slick advertising and promotion.[2] Since 1990, the US corporations have taken the lead in privatizing state-owned companies and outdated factories and asserting influence over local political leaders in the new democracies. Now in St. Petersburg, on a stroll down the famous Nevsky Prospect, you can see Camel umbrellas, Camel ashtrays, and other paraphernalia donated by RJR Nabisco to a local cafe, in exchange for an agreement that the cafe will sell only RJR's cigarettes.[3]

During the first five years of this decade, the number of smokers in Russia and the Commonwealth of Independent States reportedly grew by 5.7 percent, while rates in North America declined.[4] "The former Soviet Union is a huge, raw opportunity for us," said R.J. Reynolds International president Anthony Butterworth in 1994.[5]

The results in the table below show a sharp increase in smoking rates among young women since the tobacco transnationals moved into Ukraine. Smoking rates among women, which had been declining in the early 1980s, began to rise in the mid-1980s, but really took off in the 1990s after the entry of Philip Morris and RJR Nabisco.

TABLE VI
Prevalence of Smoking Among Women in Ukraine

	Years of Survey			
Age	1977-1978	1982-1983	1987-1988	1994-1995
20-29	7.9	7.5	12.8	31.9
30-39	7.3	7.0	10.6	23.6
40-49	3.2	3.4	6.5	19.1
50-59	2.6	2.0	3.2	7.5
20-59	5.2	5.0	8.3	20.5

Source: Institute of Cardiology (Ukraine)

Philip Morris and RJR Nabisco have used joint ventures with national cigarette or even non-tobacco companies, including Autovaz, the Russian car company, to establish a stronghold in the Russian market.[6] Philip Morris has done more investing in local cigarette factories than RJR Nabisco,[7] although RJR Nabisco has invested in Russia's largest cigarette plant in St. Petersburg and acquired controlling interest in factories in southern and central Russia, as well as two in the Ukraine.[8]

Tobacco transnationals produce at least 70 percent of cigarettes made in the Ukraine.[9] Philip Morris Inc., RJR Nabisco and Reemtsma, bought up shares in Ukraine's five largest cigarette factories and now control 75 percent of its manufacturing capacity.[10]

In 1992, RJR Nabisco was the first tobacco transnational to enter the Ukraine.[11] RJR negotiated directly with aides to the Ukrainian president to acquire a majority share in two factories—one in Kremenchuk and one in Lviv. RJR Nabisco representatives, according to Russian business people, offered as inducements to "top government officials" a set of luxury cars to help get the deal through. RJR Nabisco has denied such a deal was made.[12]

In a deal shrouded in secrecy, Philip Morris bought a majority stake in the Ukrainian cigarette factory in Kharkov in 1994.[13] Philip Morris closed the plant to Ukrainian bureaucrats and journalists, and withdrew from the Ukrainian tobacco association, Ukrtabak.[14] Philip Morris is alleged to have hired highly paid non-Ukrainian management at the plant. In 1996, Philip Morris food subsidiary Jacobs Suchard also established a presence in Ukraine by purchasing a controlling share of Trostyanets chocolate factory.[15]

Philip Morris and RJR Nabisco's jump into the Ukrainian market has proved lucrative. In 1997, analysts predicted that Ukrainian cigarette production would fall because tobacco transnationals are "flooding the market," forcing cuts in domestic production.[16] The Ukrainian government has failed to stem the influx of the Western tobacco corporations. Local production of Western brands allows transnationals to escape excise and import taxes.

Influence of US Tobacco Corporations in Ukrainian Public Health Policy

Although tobacco advertising was banned in 1992 by the "Principles of the Legislation of Ukraine on Health Protection" and confirmed in 1994 by Presidential Decree, enforcement has been inadequate and the legislation was unclear about the definition of "advertisement." The tobacco and advertising lobby persuaded the Parliament Commission on Mass Media to write a law with few restrictions on tobacco advertising. The lobby was financed by Philip Morris and other tobacco transnationals. The tobacco industry even produced a document titled "Questions and Answers on Banning Tobacco Advertising in Ukraine Prepared for the Members of Parliament in Ukraine by the Association of Independent Advisers for the Development of the Ukrainian Tobacco Industry." The document claimed that Ukraine would lose $400 million if an advertising ban were put in place,[17] $100 million in lost revenue for the advertising industry, $100 million in lost foreign tobacco investment, and $28 million in lost tax revenue, and $172 million in other revenues.

The Alcohol and Drug Information Center (ADIC) checked the Association's calculations in the document and concluded they are wrong and misleading. ADIC distributed an analysis to members of parliament about the economic and other effects of the advertising ban, that pointed out the Association assumed there would be a four-fold increase in the size of the Ukrainian tobacco crop. Recently, there have been two decreases in crop size. Not only were the calculations misleading, but the Association that produced it turned out to be nothing more than a front group. Michael Parsons, a spokesperson for Philip Morris International in Lausanne, Switzerland, later acknowledged that the document was produced by his employer.[18]

The parliament adopted the ban in March 1996 but the President issued a veto in April. When the debate continued in May, ADIC proposed a compromise resolution similar to the European directive. It is not a total ban because it allows advertisements in closed tobacco shops. It was a very hot discussion but most parliamentarians were ready to support a position that favored public health. The tobacco lobby managed to postpone a decision with strategic use of technicalities. Recognizing that the industry could not save TV and radio advertising, they prepared new legislation. When debate resumed, Speaker of the parliament Alexander Moroz, who supported the tobacco lobby, presented a "compromise" bill that was adopted without discussion. The law eventually adopted in July 1996 was significantly weaker: tobacco advertising was banned on radio and TV but allowed in print and on billboards.[19]

The Chair of the Parliament Media Commission, Mr. Victor Ponedilko, and his colleague on the Commission, Mr. Vitaliy Shevchenko, are among the political allies of the tobacco transnationals. The tobacco transnationals have many more allies, but data on political contributions are not available in Ukraine, making it difficult to uncover. The transnational tobacco corporations organize presentations and other events for members of parliament.

How Philip Morris and RJR Nabisco Get Around or Undermine Existing Regulations

At present, there is significant direct advertising on billboards and in print, as well as indirect advertising on T-shirts, plastic bags,

Cafe "Start," fully dressed in RJR Nabisco's Camel colors, is located near a sports center in Kiev. Photo by Konstantin Krasovsky, 1998.

cafe umbrellas, and little private shop lights—even trolley cars. A giant Camel logo was installed on one of the biggest buildings in Kiev. These advertisements violate advertising laws because they have no health warnings. While tobacco advertising is banned on TV, one TV channel has a special youth musical program called "Camel Rock." Tobacco ads for Marlboro, Parliament, and Vogue remain common in women's magazines.

R.J. Reynolds, in cooperation with a Kiev fashion magazine, sponsored parties in a nightclub featuring Camel posters and Camel dancing girls. The parties were videotaped and broadcast on the state television station, Camel logos and all.[20] RJR also published an ad called "Kiev Camel Fun Guide," which listed a variety of events around Kiev, including a free cartoon show for underprivileged children, athletic competitions, children's theater, and a pop music concert.[21]

In 1997, Philip Morris organized two big advertising campaigns. The first, "Marlboro Adventure Team," was premised on attracting drivers to a rally; the second was called "Win a Trip to America" and required participants to send in three empty packs of L&M cigarettes. Supposedly only persons older than 18 could participate in the two advertising campaigns, but Kiev was full of advertisements which pretended to be non-tobacco ads, opening the door to advertise to youth. First prize was a trip to the US for two. There were 9,000 other prizes such as bags, watches, and T-shirts with L&M logos in the form of an American flag. At present, Philip Morris has organized a national "Person of the Year" competition that is heavily advertised in all kinds of media. Leading newspapers and TV channels are among "information sponsors" of the competition.

In the spring of 1995, the Burnett advertising agency opened an office in Kiev just as cigarette billboard advertising was coming down because of a temporary presidential decree. While the local advertising industry did not oppose the ban[22]—national cigarette companies at present account for a very small percentage of total production and do no advertising—the transnational tobacco corporations developed a voluntary advertising code in an effort to preempt strict regulations on advertising.

In addition to influencing public health policy, the tobacco transnationals also seek to circumvent laws to promote tobacco. In a secret report by Duncan-Kiev, a Philip Morris distributor, the willingness of tobacco transnationals to depend on smuggling to market their products is alleged. As reported in the *Nezavisimost* (Independence) newspaper in 1996, "Smuggling to Ukraine is undertaken with support of the five transnational tobacco corporations (Philip Morris, Reynolds, Reetsma, BAT, Rothmans). They could stop smuggling immediately if they wished, because they know which of their clients are involved."[23]

Media Dependency on Tobacco Advertising

In May 1997, the *All-Ukrainian News* published a front page article about Philip Morris investments and increasing tobacco production, illustrating the close relationship of major media and tobacco money. Not by coincidence, the article was published on May 31, World No Tobacco Day. During the debate over the new tobacco advertising law, most media supported the tobacco industry because they expected revenue from tobacco advertising. Deputy editor of the parliament newspaper, *Voice of Ukraine,* Mr. Leonid Brovchenko published a piece blaming ad-ban proponents for receiving international support which, he said, threatened the domestic tobacco industry, even though the domestic industry barely exists because of foreign investment. The major tobacco factories are 90 percent joint ventures that use mostly imported machinery and tobacco. In this way, Ukrainian smokers contribute to the profits of the tobacco transnationals and the economies of foreign countries. In the same issue, the same journalist published an article about happy Ukrainian smokers that can smoke legal—not smuggled— Marlboro and L&Ms.

Tobacco control activists encountered difficulty in getting their message out during the parliamentary debate about the tobacco ad ban. US-financed Radio Liberty accepts no tobacco advertising and ADIC was able to get some publicity that way, but attempts to get an article published about Philip Morris marketing and promotional tactics proved very difficult. Several newspapers responded that they could publish it only as a paid advertisement, which had never happened to ADIC before.

Lessons for the US

The US tobacco settlement negotiated in June 1997, and currently being debated creates the illusion that the "tobacco problem" can be settled. But outside the US, the litigation process is hardly possible. The US should follow international models like Canada, Australia, and other pioneers of tobacco control.

NOTES

1   James Rupert and Glenn Frankel, "In Ex-Soviet Markets, U.S. Brands Took on Role of Capitalist Liberator," *Washington Post*, Nov. 19, 1996.

2   Emil Tsenov, "Russia, Ukraine, and the Czech Republic Cigarette Markets," *Tobacco International*, June 1997, p. 52.

3   "Biggies Try to Sell Homegrown Products," *Tobacco International*, Oct. 1997, p. 22.

4   "Drastic Decline in Cigarette Imports Predicted for Russia," *Tobacco Reporter*, Winter 1998, p. 9.

5   Paul Klebnikov, "Opiate of the Masses," *Forbes*, April 11, 1994, p. 74.

6   Emil Tsenov, "Progress and Potential: Russia, Ukraine, and the Czech Republic Cigarette Markets," *Tobacco International*., p. 52.

7   Suein Hwang, "RJR to Cut Staff by 10%, Post Charge Mostly for International Tobacco Unit," *Wall Street Journal*, Dec. 17, 1997.

8   "Multinational Investment," *Tobacco Reporter*, Winter 1998, p. 37.

9   Emil Tsenov, "Progress and Potential: Russia, Ukraine, and the Czech Republic Cigarette Markets," *Tobacco International*, June 1997, p. 54 reports 70 percent of local production is by Western tobacco transnationals. However, the State Statistics Committee of Ukraine puts the figure at 92 percent.

10 Rupert and Frankel, "In Ex-Soviet Markets, US Brands Took on Role of Capitalist Liberator," *Washington Post,* Nov. 19, 1996.

11 Glenn John, "An Independent Approach to Independence, *Tobacco International,* November 1, 1993, p. 28.

12 Paul Klebnikov, "Opiate of the Masses," *Forbes*, April 11, 1994, p. 75.

13 "Philip Morris Buys Stake in Ukraine Cigarette Plant," *Wall Street Journal*, May 31, 1994; Emil Tsenov, "Russia, Ukraine, and the Czech Republic Cigarette Markets," *Tobacco Interna-*

tional, June 1997, p. 52.

14 *Kiev Post*, Aug. 15-21, 1996.

15 *Zerkalo Nedeli* (Mirror of the Week), Ukraine, March 15, 1997.

16 "Ukraine: Imports Choke Homegrown Cigarette Makers," *Tobacco International,* June 1997, p. 4.

17 Rupert and Frankel, "In Ex-Soviet Markets, U.S. Brands Took on Role of Capitalist Liberator," *Washington Post,* Nov. 19, 1996.

18 Rupert and Frankel, "In Ex-Soviet Markets, U.S. Brands Took on Role of Capitalist Liberator," *Washington Post,* Nov. 19, 1996.

19 *Tobacco or Health in Ukraine*, ADIC-Ukraine, 1997.

20 Rupert and Frankel, "In Ex-Soviet Markets, U.S. Brands Took on Role of Capitalist Liberator,"*Washington Post,* Nov. 19, 1996.

21 "Kiev Camel Fund Guide" advertising supplement.

22 Rupert and Frankel, "In Ex-Soviet Markets, U.S. Brands Took on Role of Capitalist Liberator," *Washington Post,* Nov. 19, 1996.

23 *Nezavisimost* (Independence) newspaper (Ukraine), Oct. 22, 1996.

Malaysia: A Case Study in Brand Stretching

by Mary Assunta, Consumers Association of Penang

Malaysia provides a good example of why one should not compromise with the cigarette industry and consult with it when drawing up tobacco control programs. Malaysia can also provide many examples of how cigarette companies can circumvent a ban on direct cigarette advertising.

Malaysia has a multi-ethnic, multi-religious population of 20 million. Sixty percent of the adult male and only 5 percent of the female population smoke.[1] The tobacco market is dominated by foreign multinationals and growing at the rate of about 2 percent annually. The top three cigarette manufacturers are Rothmans of Pall Mall, 55 percent; R.J. Reynolds Berhad, 18 percent; and Malaysian Tobacco Company (subsidiary of BAT), 15 percent.[2] Together they spend about US$ 89 million a year in advertisements in various media and in sponsorship activities in Malaysia.[3] RJR Nabisco is the fourth largest advertiser in Malaysia.[4]

While the tobacco industry in the US is faced with declining sales, mounting court action, and well-organized public pressure, here in Malaysia the US tobacco corporations are unfazed by these developments. They continue to step up their already aggressive promotions and devise even more innovative and creative ways of hooking young people.

Some of the strategies used by the US companies to attract new smokers among young Malaysians, to keep the smokers smoking, and to establish a social acceptance among the rest of the Malaysian public are highlighted here.

Background on the US Tobacco Corporations in Malaysia

R.J. Reynolds Tobacco Company owns 60 percent of the issues capital of R.J. Reynolds Berhad.[5] RJR Berhad has a market share

84

of 18 percent and is reported to be the fastest growing cigarette manufacturer.[6] It sells brands such as Salem, Winston, More, and Camel. Salem is the second largest selling brand in Malaysia[7] and occupies ten percent of the local market. In 1997, RJR Berhad reported a major expansion program in opening a new plant for the production of finished cigarettes for export to affiliate companies in Asia.[8]

Philip Morris's Marlboro cigarettes used to be imported directly from the US. As of 1997, they are manufactured locally by Philip Morris (M) Sdn. Bhd. Malaysia now exports Marlboro to Thailand.[9]

The average Malaysian does not associate food products such as Kraft with tobacco. Philip Morris's Kraft is popular among the Malaysian public and outlets are found throughout the country. Kraft cheese is an established brand of cheese.

Tobacco Control Legislation in Malaysia

Malaysia has regulations placing restrictions on the sale and marketing of cigarettes, and smoking in certain public places is banned. The Control of Tobacco Products Regulations 1993 prohibits the direct advertising of tobacco products in the local media, bans distribution of free samples of cigarettes, bans vending machines, and prohibits those under 18 from smoking or purchasing cigarettes.[10] However, it does not prohibit tobacco corporations from using cigarette brand names to advertise other products and services. This has given the tobacco transnationals a convenient loophole to exploit. Malaysia probably serves as the worst example of how this loophole can be exploited to the maximum by the tobacco corporations.

Since direct cigarette advertisements were banned over television in 1982, the tobacco corporations got around this ban by going into trademark diversification and began selling a lifestyle involving clothes, travels, clubs, etc. with cigarette brands. This form of advertising is commonly referred to as indirect advertising or "brand stretching." So R.J. Reynolds has one travel company in Kuala Lumpur, but spends millions advertising its service on national television and billboards placed all over the country. The tobacco corporations say it is a legitimate business and refer to it as "trademark diversification advertising."[11] The public, however, sees it as a front to advertise cigarette brands on television, although such ads are banned.

Malaysia is a good testing ground for the tobacco corporations to employ new tactics in indirect advertising and to circumvent bans and restrictions successfully. We believe it is practiced to an extent matched nowhere else in the world.

In 1992, R.J. Reynolds was exposed for advertising a nonexistent travel business daily on television—Salem High Country.[12] One could not go on a Salem High Country tour because there was no such package in reality. Although an official complaint was registered with the authorities to act against the corporation for false advertising, no action was taken.[13]

Although direct cigarette advertisements are prohibited, the tobacco corporations are the largest advertising and sponsorship spenders, occupying some 25 percent of the total advertising expenditures for 1995.[14] The government-owned Radio Television Malaysia earns 43 percent of its revenue from advertisements placed by tobacco corporations—about US$ 33 million.[15]

At the 13th Asia-Pacific Cancer Conference in 1996, the Malaysian Minister of Health stated the Health Ministry had given up hopes of getting the tobacco corporations to voluntarily stop indirect advertising. He said the corporations had instead intensified their promotions and sponsorship. He said, "We are doing our best (to save people) but at the same time, the cigarette companies are intensifying their campaigns through promotions and sponsorship."[16] Earlier he admitted that the nation is fighting a losing battle with tobacco companies and is facing a smoking epidemic.[17]

Advertising and Promotional Tactics Used by the US Tobacco Corporations in Malaysia

Music, sports, and adventure appeal to the young. Throw in some style, fun, an attitude, and some macho-toughness, and you have all the right ingredients to attract the young.

MUSIC

R.J. Reynolds Berhad operates a record shop called the Salem Power Station.[18] The Salem brand has been prominent in sponsoring live pop concerts in the cities, and music concerts over television under the "Salem Cool Planet" banner. These events are heavily advertised over television, radio, and newspapers. The advertisements claim the event is "where the music comes alive." RJR sponsors live concerts and brings in international stars popular with young people, such as Alanis Morissette, Hootie & the Blowfish, and Paula Abdul.

RJR Nabisco operates a music shop called the Salem Power Station in Malaysia. The Salem logo and colors are identical to its tobacco brand.

R.J. Reynolds chooses entertainers that appeal to the young because they have controversial images, defy the conventional, and rebel against acceptable norms. The Salem concerts, which are usually held in Kuala Lumpur, are well attended by young people. Aggressive advertising for these concerts, especially on television, starts well before the event itself and appears many times a day, especially during prime time.

When a concert is organized in Malaysia, R.J. Reynolds also sponsors a radio program where listeners can call in and answer trivia questions about the pop stars and win free tickets to their concert. RJR would also sponsor contests through newspaper ads for free tickets. Since tickets to such concerts are usually pricey, young people are eager to win a free ticket to see their favorite entertainer. In the past, the winner had to go to a "Salem booth" to collect the ticket.[19] Free cigarettes used to be handed out to the audience attending the Salem-sponsored events. The distribution of free samples has since been outlawed.

R.J. Reynolds also sponsors the "Cool Planet Chart" show on television, which gives the latest update on international pop music. But not all Malaysian teenagers enjoy Western pop music. To cater to Chinese youth, Salem also sponsors live concerts or music programs on television featuring such Chinese entertainers as Daniel Chan and Fay Wong.

Other promotional tactics under "Salem Cool Planet" include the "Blockbuster Spotlight," where free tickets to blockbuster movies, such as *Face Off, Air Force One, My Best Friend's Wedding, Nothing to Lose, The Assignment* and *Excess Baggage* are distributed. All one needs to do is take the newspaper advertisement for the promotion to the participating cinemas at certain advertised times and redeem it for two free tickets.[20] R.J. Reynolds also organizes year-end disco parties under the "Salem Cool Planet" banner, previously called "Salem Celebrations."[21] Free tickets to the parties can be won by sticking Salem car stickers (distributed free at gas stations) in a creative manner on your car. Salem Cool Planet paraphernalia such as coasters are also found in discos.

Two Malaysian newspaper advertisments show how RJR Nabisco uses sponsorship to promote tobacco with its 1997 Salem Cool Planet ad promoting the ATP (tennis) tour, and a 1996 Salem Celebration ad promoting a party, dance, and music.

SPORTS

Like other tobacco corporations operating in Malaysia, R.J. Reynolds is also into sports, and Salem has found its niche in sponsoring tennis. RJR sponsors tennis tournaments or the telecasts of major tennis tournaments. This way it gets to associate the Salem brand name with tennis champions, with intensive television advertising. While tennis may not be the most popular sport among

Malaysians (soccer is the favorite national game and is controlled by Dunhill sponsorship), nevertheless the advertising mileage on television is phenomenal.

Winston World of Action sponsors television programs on wrestling and boxing.[22] As a sport, wrestling is not well developed in Malaysia; however, the sport has a large television audience, including children. In 1997, RJR brought wrestlers from the World Wrestling Federation to perform in several large towns in Malaysia.

Philip Morris has a long history of Marlboro sponsorship of motor racing in Malaysia. The nation's quest to host Formula One racing has certainly given Marlboro a special place in the development of this event. Meanwhile, Marlboro hosts and sponsors other motor racing events and its telecasts on television. Every Sunday afternoon Marlboro used to sponsor the Marlboro Total Malaysian Club Prix. Marlboro's sponsorship of motor racing has been endorsed by no less than Malaysia's king, prime minister, and the deputy prime minister. The Marlboro Malaysian Grand Prix in April 1997 was flagged off by the prime minister.[23]

ADVENTURE

R.J. Reynolds introduced Joe Camel into the Malaysian market in the 1980s, but it does not appear anymore. Camel is now synonymous with the "ultimate adventure" event and adventure gear that goes with the action. The image portrayed by this brand is one of a tough man, conquering the treacherous wilds—not for the faint-hearted. The Camel Trophy is another well-publicized event organized under the Camel brand name. It is also advertised over TV.

In 1993, the Camel Trophy event was held in East Malaysia and described as "the world's toughest most-exciting off-road challenge . . . 1,000 gruelling miles into the heart of Sabah." Although participants in the event are adults, the sense of adventure and nature portrayed in the advertisements is appealing to children and young people.[24]

CLOTHING

Salem, Camel, Winston, and Marlboro have all gone into trademark clothing and apparel to be able to advertise the brand name in the local mass media. Salem's line of clothes is appropriately named "Salem Attitude" and Camel's "Adventure Gear." Marlboro is called "Marlboro Classic." Color themes of the advertisements for these clothes coincide with the colors of the cigarette packets.

Fashion

with

a Fresh

New

Attitude

R.J. Reynolds promotes its tobacco trademark in this ad for Salem clothing.[25]

This 1996 Marlboro Adventure Team brochure from Indonesia advertises dates and places to find Marlboro Adventure Team stands at local shopping plazas and supermarkets where Marlboro T-shirts, lighters, jackets, and watches would be available.

MEMENTOS/SOUVENIRS

Most tobacco corporations invariably have T-shirts, caps, mugs, umbrellas, lighters, and other paraphernalia with their names and logos on them. Some are given away free at specific occasions, like sports events, while many more are sold to the public from booths built within major shopping complexes.[26]

While it is an offense for children under 18 to buy cigarettes, it is not uncommon for children under 18 to have paraphernalia of tobacco corporations. Marlboro seems to be a popular brand with boys.

At an informal workshop for student smokers from a secondary school in Penang in September 1997, it was revealed that they all have tried Marlboro cigarettes. Three of them own Marlboro T-shirts and almost all of them own Marlboro stickers, four of them own Marlboro caps, five of them own Marlboro bags, six of them own Marlboro lighters. The legal age for purchasing cigarettes is above 18 years. At age 14, this group of about 25 boys are all smokers and they belong to the Fresh Breath club which was initiated to help them quit.[27]

A Marlboro gear stand in a shopping complex in Malaysia. Marlboro jackets, backpacks, hats, and an umbrella are on display, along with posters for Marlboro World of Sports. Photo courtesy of Consumers Association of Penang, 1997.

The Tobacco Regulations of 1993 also omitted foreign publications from observing the direct advertisement ban. Magazines such as *Time* and *Newsweek*, and other imported periodicals may carry cigarette advertisements, although the same magazines circulated in countries with total bans such as Singapore do not contain these ads. For example, the March 10, 1997, issues of *Time* and *Newsweek* sold in Malaysia had an advertisement for Marlboro on the back page, with no health warning. The same issue sold in Singapore, where cigarette advertising is banned, does not have a Marlboro advertisement.

The Influence of the US Tobacco Corporations in Malaysia

The tobacco corporations in Malaysia usually conduct their lobbying activities through the Confederation of Malaysian Tobacco Manufacturers (CMTM). While the settlement issue was being hotly debated in the US in 1997, in Malaysia the CMTM pooled together US$ 280,000 and launched an anti-smoking campaign in collaboration with the Ministry of Education in some 1,500 secondary schools throughout the country between May and August. The campaign theme (as in the US) is "Right Decisions Right Now."[28]

The timing of the campaign was significant in that it took place about the same time the US settlement issue was released, so that the US tobacco corporations would not have to answer to charges in Malaysia. It also coincided precisely with the controversial Peter Stuyvesant KRU concert tour whose advertisements were more aggressive and attractive and contrasted sharply with the preachy, unattractive anti-smoking ones placed sparingly by CMTM's campaign.

Although the launch of the campaign received much publicity in the local press, in the following months a check with secondary schools in Penang revealed that there was no real campaign activity on the ground. This campaign by the CMTM and the Education Ministry's endorsement was criticized by the public health community.

The government has been criticized for compromising with the tobacco lobby. The lack of seriousness in addressing the promotion of tobacco, particularly indirect advertisements and sports sponsorship, has been highlighted many times. The tobacco lobby seems to have found a supporter in Malaysia's minister of information, who has indicated that the government's television-radio station cannot do without tobacco money.[29] Hence the contradictions and compromises continue.

The Information Ministry's support of the tobacco industry seems to have a direct bearing on the electronic media's policy on tobacco. While tobacco-related illnesses are increasing,[30] and the minister of health has declared that the nation is facing a smoking epidemic, there are no regular anti-smoking messages aired over radio or television in Malaysia.

Lessons for the US

WHAT THE US CORPORATIONS CANNOT DO AT HOME, THEY SHOULD NOT DO OVERSEAS

The transnational tobacco corporations always argue that they do not break the law and follow the rules and regulations of the country they are operating in. In reality, laws in developing countries are often weaker, nonexistent, or indifferently enforced, so the corporations engage in activities not allowed at home. For example, no warnings are included on their cigarette advertisements, or higher levels of nicotine and tar are used. Or, as is often the case, the foreign companies lobby against stringent laws to prevent them from being enacted.

At a minimum, the US tobacco corporations should follow the laws they are subject to at home. If the laws of the country they are operating in are more stringent, they should follow the laws of that land.

LIFE OUTSIDE THE US IS NOT LESS VALUABLE THAN LIFE IN THE US

What is hazardous for Americans is also hazardous for the rest of the world. Restrictions and standards in the US should be followed by the US corporations operating overseas. These corporations should not, for example, sell US cigarette brands with higher tar and nicotine levels than those sold in the US. This amounts to a double standard, and in the past the tobacco corporations have been notorious for practicing such double standards. If nicotine is classified as an addictive drug in the US, and labeled as such, all US tobacco corporations selling their cigarettes overseas should label them accordingly.

HEALTH BEFORE PROFITS: PUBLIC HEALTH AND SAFETY SHOULD BE PUT ABOVE ECONOMIC GAINS

The US government should not use the "free trade" argument and the threat of unilateral trade sanctions (under Section 301 of its 1974 Trade Act) to force open markets especially in Asian countries, as it has done in the past with Thailand, South Korea, Taiwan, and Japan. The US government, in the face of developments with the tobacco industry in the US, should extend its tobacco control policies overseas and force its tobacco corporations to comply with US standards in all of their operations.

HALT OVERSEAS EXPANSION

Although the settlement being negotiated in 1997 in the US is referred to as a "Global Settlement," it is not global in reality. The proposal does not address the behavior of US tobacco corporations overseas. The settlement does not offer the international population any protection or compensation similar to that being proposed for US citizens. Because US tobacco corporations are global in their operations, the settlement should address the implications for overseas markets. Whatever gains the US citizens derive out of a legislated settlement will be lost in the rest of the world where people are already faced with increased marketing and promotion of this deadly product by the very same tobacco corporations.

It has been reported that Big Tobacco has "flatly refused to negotiate" on international tobacco control issues.[31] The US government has to remember that the US accounts for only 4 percent of the world tobacco markets. This means 96 percent of cigarette sales are generated outside the US.[32] This in itself warrants responsibility from the US government to address the overseas operations of the US tobacco transnationals.

There should be a moratorium to stop overseas expansion of markets by the US tobacco corporations. The US government should be consistent in its public health policies, domestically and internationally. In this case, its firm stand to curb smoking among its citizens should be reflected in its international trade policies.

NOTES

1   "Puff Until You Snuff," *Sunday Mail*, Dec. 21, 1997.

2   "When Profits Have Final Say," *New Straits Times* (Malaysia),

May 31, 1997.

3   "When Profits Have Final Say," *New Straits Times* (Malaysia), May 31, 1997. US$1=RM4.5.

4   "Top 10 Marketers in 56 Countries," *Advertising Age International*, Nov. 1997, p. 10.

5   R.J. Reynolds Berhad Annual Report 1995, p. 35.

6   R.J. Reynolds Berhad Annual Report 1996, Summary Analysis, p. 1.

7   R.J. Reynolds Berhad Annual Report 1995, p. 8.

8   S. Retna, "Cigarette Maker to Introduce More Brands," *Sun* (Malaysia), May 15, 1997.

9   "PMI Plant Gets Government Nod," *Tobacco Reporter*, May 1994, p. 7 (SCARCNet Summary); the author has a box of Marlboro purchased in Thailand, and printed on the box is "made by Philip Morris (Malaysia) Sdn Bhd."

10   Esther Tan, "More Checks on Errant Smokers and Firms," *New Straits Times* (Malaysia), Sept. 30, 1996.

11   Kang Siew Li, "No Immediate Plans for Tobacco Ad Clampdown," *Business Times*, Aug. 14, 1996.

12   "Bogus 'Salem High Country' Holiday," *Utusan Konsumer* (Malaysia), mid-September, 1992.

13   An official from Consumers Association of Penang (CAP) wanted to go on a tour to Mt. Cook and Jasper, which were two destinations advertised on television, but there were no tours to these places by the travel company. CAP sent a letter to the authorities urging them to take action against the corporation under the Trade Description Act 1972 for false advertising.

14   Adeline Ong, "Tobacco Companies' Ads to Remain," *Business Times* (Malaysia), Aug. 27, 1996.

15   Adeline Ong, "Tobacco Companies' Ads to Remain," *Business Times* (Malaysia), Aug. 27, 1996.

16   J. Sebastian, "Chua: Calls Go Unheeded by Cigarette Firms," *Star* (Malaysia), Nov. 18, 1996.

17   *Sun* (Malaysia), Sept. 7, 1996.

18 R.J. Reynolds Berhad Annual Report 1995, p. 26.

19 "Salem Targets Women and Youths," *Utusan Konsumer* (Malaysia), mid-Sept., 1992.

20 As advertised in *The Star* (Malaysia), Oct. 18, 1997. Condition: one must be 18 years and above to get the tickets.

21 "Salem Targets Women and Youths," *Utusan Konsumer* (Malaysia), mid-Sept., 1992.

22 Winston World of Action advertisement, *The Star* (Malaysia), Feb. 25, 1998.

23 "Prime Minister to Flag Off Glamour Race," *New Straits Times* (Malaysia), April 8, 1997; "Dr. M Opens Malaysian Grand Prix," *The Star* (Malaysia), April 14, 1997.

24 Camel Trophy ad, *The Star* (Malaysia), Nov. 4, 1992.

25 *The Star*, Dec. 12, 1996, p.19. Copyright by R.J. Reynolds.

26 Dr. Zarihah M. Zain, Ministry of Health (Malaysia) and Mary Assunta (Consumers Association of Penang), "Circumvention of Bans on Direct Advertising," (paper presented at the 10th World Conference on Tobacco or Health), Beijing, Aug. 1997.

27 The workshop was conducted by the Consumers Association of Penang, Sept. 1997; Jennifer Lin, "Cigarette Wars," *The Philadelphia Inquirer*, Dec. 18, 1997.

28 Frederick Fernandez, "Anti-Smoking Blitz at 1,500 Schools," *Sunday Star* (Malaysia), May 18, 1997; Zazali Musa, "'No Hidden Agenda' in Anti-Smoking Drive," *The Star* (Malaysia), May 24, 1997.

29 "Gov't Softens Stand on Smoking Ban," *Business Times* (Malaysia), Feb. 14, 1997.

30 Vijayan Menon, "More Places to Be Made No-Smoking Zones," *New Strait Times* (Malaysia), Nov. 8, 1996.

31 Carol McGruder, "Big Tobacco Targets the World's Poor," *Utusan Konsumer* (Malaysia), mid-Aug., 1997.

32 Carol McGruder, "Big Tobacco Targets the World's Poor," *Utusan Konsumer* (Malaysia), mid-Aug., 1997.

THE GLOBAL IMPLICATIONS
OF A US SETTLEMENT WITH
TOBACCO CORPORATIONS

[I]t's natural to expect that the [tobacco] companies will try to, you know, accelerate the growing markets [in Asia and Eastern Europe]. And . . . if they're dangerous to children here, they're dangerous to children there . . . it is as inevitable as the sun coming out today that international institutions will be called upon and nations will be called upon to responsibly deal with this. — *President Clinton, White House Press Conference, August 7, 1997* [1]

Most important, the agreement secures the tobacco industry's rightful place in the mainstream of legitimate U.S. commerce. — *Steven Goldstone, CEO of RJR Nabisco*[2]

Since 1996, the US tobacco corporations have aggressively pursued a legislated solution to avoid full implementation of the US Food and Drug Administration regulations, to free them from future liability, to maximize their stock values, and to free up resources to focus on expanding into international tobacco markets. Internal documents from Philip Morris show that as far back as 1993 the corporation considered pursuing some limited advertising ban legislation as a strategy to fend off tobacco control efforts and to boost the corporation's image.[3] In May 1996, Philip Morris did advance a legislative proposal but was met with public skepticism and outrage.[4] As Philip Morris drew criticism for driving up the cost of our elections and drowning out voices of ordinary people, not even Congressional allies like Representative Tom Bliley (VA) or Senator Wendell Ford (KY) dared introduce the Philip Morris-drafted bill.

In 1997, the US tobacco corporations negotiated a deal with all but one of the US state attorneys general who are suing the industry to recover health care costs to treat tobacco-related illnesses. The industry is seeking immunity from future liability, as well as creating additional hurdles for the FDA to regulate tobacco. The industry trade journal *Tobacco International* states:

> However, one positive result of the agreement for tobacco companies is it gives the industry certainty. The stock market likes certainty. . . . Now that this "uniquely American" accord has been reached, there should be more predictability in the industry's future—one free of the threat of an overnight attack from the anti-tobacco forces.[5]

And in a later issue, the same journal observed that "without the proposed settlement in hand, tobacco industry leaders must focus on courtroom battles rather than on the business of selling cigarettes."[6] Some form of legislation is expected in the US in 1998.

International public health advocates at the 10th World Conference on Tobacco or Health in Beijing in August 1997 were virtually unanimous in their opposition to a US deal with the tobacco corporations. Most saw the proposed deal with the attorneys general of states suing the tobacco corporations as an opportunity for the tobacco giants to focus more aggressively on expanding into overseas markets. The fear among many people working on tobacco control outside the US is that the rest of the world will be left to fend for itself against the US-based tobacco corporations once the US public believes the problem at home is solved. The deal could also impose limitations on lawsuits filed outside the US.

Phil Carlton, a lobbyist for the tobacco corporations, said in a statement regarding the international implications of the proposed deal with the US tobacco corporations that the US cannot make laws for other countries, but the tobacco industry would be willing to discuss tobacco policy with any government that asks.[7]

> [The] settlement is just a new way of expansion of the tobacco industry to other countries. — *Konstantin Krasovsky, Alcohol and Drug Information Center, Ukraine*[8]

Delegates to the 10th World Conference on Tobacco or Health passed a resolution in response to the proposed deal in the US, urging all governments to "consider the international implications of tobacco control policies and settlements with the tobacco industry," to ensure that the tobacco industry pay the costs of damage caused by tobacco. The resolution stated that actions taken by individual countries should "not contribute to an increase in the worldwide epidemic of tobacco-related disease and death," that the rights of those not party to a settlement should not be traded away, and that measures "do not inhibit full public scrutiny of the past, present and future activities of the tobacco industry."[9]

NOTES

1   "Excerpts from Clinton's News Conference at the White House," *New York Times,* Aug. 7, 1997 (SCARCNet summary).

2   "Big Tobacco Speaks Out on the Proposed Tobacco Settlement," *Multinational Monitor,* July/Aug. 1997, p. 2.

3   Barry Meier, "Philip Morris Considered Proposing Ad Curbs in '93" *New York Times,* Jan. 7, 1998.

4   Ira Teinowitz, "PM Moves To Dodge Regulation," *Advertising Age,* May 20, 1996, p. 63.

5   Jane Shea, "TI Editorial," *Tobacco International,* July 1997, p. 3.

6   Jane Shea, "TI Editorial," *Tobacco International,* July 1997, p. 3.

7   Nancy Stancill, "Saving the Farm," *Charlotte Observer,* Oct. 21, 1997.

8   Response to INFACT survey from the 10th World Conference on Tobacco or Health, Beijing, Aug. 1997.

9   "Resolutions of the 10th World Conference on Tobacco or Health," Beijing, Aug. 1997.

CONSUMER PRESSURE AS A KEY COUNTERMEASURE TO TOBACCO PROMOTION

INFACT's Tobacco Industry Boycott and the growing liability of the association of food with tobacco is having an impact on the performance of Philip Morris's and RJR Nabisco's food businesses. This liability can be effectively leveraged to bring about changes in the expansion of the tobacco industry internationally, as well as to pressure the industry to meet INFACT's Public Challenge.

Overall, the US tobacco corporations' food businesses have been fairly stagnant in the US, lagging behind the food industry as a whole.[1] Nabisco's performance has been especially poor, and Philip Morris's food revenues have fallen far short of analyst predictions. Philip Morris has also increased its advertising, with a huge jump in 1994.[2] Post (cereals) and Maxwell House (coffee), two of the products targeted by INFACT's boycott, have increased image advertising substantially, and shifted from promotion of the product to promoting corporate philanthropy. According to Professor James Post, an expert in marketing at Boston University's School of Management, the tobacco corporations "recognize their image is at risk, and they are clearly trying to bolster that image through corporate citizenship."[3]

Nabisco's Nicotine Addiction Takes Toll on Food Business

Analysts estimate that per share value of RJR Nabisco's food division would increase by 127 percent if freed from the tobacco corporation.[4] Nabisco has disappointed projections of double-digit growth, and earnings have fallen short of expectations, according to the corporation's own Annual Reports and statements by top corporate executives.[5]

In 1996, a shareholder resolution filed by the Interfaith Center on Corporate Responsibility, calling for an immediate Nabisco spinoff, received 38 percent support—unprecedented for a social issues resolution.[6]

In 1994, "people were assuming [Nabisco] could jump 40 feet." Now, according to one stock analyst, "they have lowered it to four feet."[7] Following former Nabisco CEO John Greeniaus's 1995 prediction that "this company's glory years still lie ahead. . . . No food company has more new product momentum," RJR Nabisco's domestic food profits fell by 54 percent in two years.[8] Worldwide, profits from food are down 24 percent since 1993, the year before INFACT's boycott began.[9] Yet Nabisco is of greater importance to the corporation than tobacco, as RJR Nabisco now derives more than half of its total revenues from food.[10] Nabisco has increased advertising spending to shore up core products like SnackWell's and Oreos.[11]

Prior to 1994, Nabisco's closest competitors were losing ground in market share to Nabisco. Since 1994, that trend has been reversed.[12] In 1997, Nabisco cookie sales fell almost 4 percent, while its closest rival's sales rose 2 percent, prodding one analyst from Goldman, Sachs & Company to observe that "they didn't stay ahead of the competition."[13]

Philip Morris's Tobacco Business Spoils Kraft Foods

Philip Morris's North American food revenues have declined significantly from $21.5 billion in 1994 to $16.4 billion in 1996, in part due to the sell-off of portions of the Kraft Foods division.[14] Kraft's divestitures may also be linked to the liability of the tobacco business. The only growth in food revenues over 1994 has been in the international sector. International tobacco sales have since overtaken North American food as the largest single segment of revenue for the corporation.[15]

At the beginning of 1994, financial projections for Philip Morris suggested the corporation would derive nearly 60 percent of its revenues from food by 1997, 22 percent from international tobacco sales, and 12 percent from US tobacco sales, with the remainder coming from its beer and financial services segments.[16] The actual results at the end of 1996 show the corporation is on a substantially different course.

TABLE VII
Philip Morris 1997 Financial Projections v. 1996
Results by Business Segment
(in $ billions)

Business Segment	Net Revenue Projected for 1997 (in 1994)	1996 Net Revenue (Actual)	Operating Income Projected for 1997 (in 1994)	1996 Operating Income (Actual)
Domestic Tobacco	7.5	12.5	2.8	4.2
Int'l Tobacco	13.3	24.1	4.2	4.1
N. American Food	24.6	16.4	2.7	2.6
International Food	11.9	11.5	1.8	1.3
Beer	3.6	4.3	0.4	0.4
Financial and Real Estate	0.5	0.4	0.3	0.2
TOTAL	61.4	69.2	12.2	12.8

Source: Philip Morris Inc.–Company Reports, G.D. Black, et. al., Sanford C. Bernstein & Co., Inc., Oct. 15, 1993, pp. 6-7; Philip Morris 1996 Annual Report, pp. 24, 26.

Profits from Philip Morris's US food sales have remained fairly flat since 1994, growing by a total of only 3.5 percent from 1994-1996.[17] Philip Morris's performance falls short of analyst predictions in 1993 of 7-9 percent annual growth in North American food profits, and 5-7 percent yearly growth in North American food revenues.[18] In 1994, North American food revenues grew by just 2.9 percent, in 1995 by 3.4 percent, and just 3.8 percent in 1996 (excluding divested businesses).[19]

These are indications of the impact of consumer pressure on Philip Morris and RJR Nabisco. Boycotts are effective when they involve millions of people acting in concert, they are part of a strategic campaign, and they affect a corporation's bottom line. The efficacy of a boycott is measured not only in lost sales, but in the impact on the corporation's public image, one of its most valuable assets. Kraft and Nabisco provide Philip Morris and RJR Nabisco with legitimacy and influence they otherwise would not have. INFACT's consumer boycott connects their food and tobacco businesses, reducing the tobacco giants' ability to hide behind their food businesses.

Transnational corporations depend on consumer support to succeed. By using this power in an organized effort with others around the world, we can bring about change to prevent the needless deaths of millions of people each year.

NOTES

1   "Fortune 1000 Ranked Within Industries," *Fortune,* April 28, 1997, p. F-51; "Fortune 1000 Ranked Within Industries," *Fortune,* April 29, 1996, p. F-51; "Fortune 1000 Ranked Within Industries," *Fortune,* May 15, 1995, p. F-51; Philip Morris 1996 Annual Report, p. 26; RJR Nabisco 1996 Annual Report, p. 30.

2   "Top 10 Companies by 1994 Ad Spending," *Advertising Age International,* May 1, 1995; "100 Leading National Advertisers," *Advertising Age International,* Sept. 28, 1994, p. 4; "100 Leaders by U.S. Advertising Spending," *Advertising Age International,* Sept. 30, 1996, p. s4.

3   Personal communication with Professor Jim Post, Boston University School of Management, Oct. 16, 1997.

4   Andrew Serwer, "Who's Afraid of Carl Icahn?," *Fortune,* Feb. 17, 1997, pp. 106-107.

5   RJR Nabisco 1996 Annual Report, pp. 22-23; Andrew Serwer, "Who's Afraid of Carl Icahn?," *Fortune,* Feb. 17, 1997, pp. 104-108; Maria Mooshil, "Earnings Slide for Cigarette Firms May Be Ending After First Quarter," *Wall Street Journal,* April 11, 1994; RJR Nabisco Holdings Corp.–Company Report, B.M. Ziegler, A.G. Edwards & Sons, Inc., Jan. 18, 1994.

6   *Investor's Tobacco Reporter,* IRRC, July 1997.

7   John R. Dorfman and Yumiko One, "Steady Nabisco Might Prove, in a Slump, Crumbly as a Ritz," *Wall Street Journal,* Oct. 4, 1996.

8   RJR Nabisco Annual Report 1995, pp. 12-13.

9   RJR Nabisco 1993 Annual Report, p. 1; RJR Nabisco 1996 Annual Report, p. 30.

10 RJR Nabisco 1996 Annual Report, p. 30.

11 Yumiko Ono, "SnackWell's Puts Stress on Taste, Not Low Fat, in New Campaign," *Wall Street Journal,* Sept. 8, 1997.

12 *Market Share Reporter*–1998, pp. 61, 62, 68, 78; RJR Nabisco Holdings Corp.–Company Report, B.M. Ziegler, A.G. Edwards & Sons, Inc., Jan. 18, 1994.

13 Suein Hwang, "At Nabisco, the New Chief Walks Into a Hot

Kitchen," *Wall Street Journal,* February 5, 1998, p. B3.

14 Philip Morris 1996 Annual Report, p. 26.

15 Philip Morris 1996 Annual Report, pp. 21, 26.

16 Philip Morris Inc.–Company Reports, G.D. Black, et. al., Sanford C. Bernstein & Co., Inc., Oct. 15, 1993, pp. 6-7

17 Philip Morris 1996 Annual Report, p. 2.

18 Philip Morris Companies, Inc.–Company Report by E. Goldman, Painewebber, Inc., Sept. 2, 1993.

19 Philip Morris 1995 Annual Report, p. 23; Philip Morris 1996 Annual Report, p. 26.

THE NEED FOR GLOBAL ACTION TO HALT EXPANSION BY THE TOBACCO TRANSNATIONALS

The tobacco epidemic is driven by transnational corporations; therefore many problems created by this industry require a global solution. The World Health Organization is proposing international action for tobacco control by the year 2000 in the form of an International Framework Convention.[1] A Framework Convention is a legally binding treaty under international law, with a general statement of goals. Precedents include the 1979 Convention on Transboundary Air Pollution and the 1992 Framework Convention on Climate Change.[2] The need for action by the World Health Organization is apparent with the increasing aggressiveness of tobacco corporations' marketing to developing countries. The number of deaths is on the rise, many countries have legislation that is either weak or not enforced, and the current climate is right to mobilize policy makers to get behind the international tobacco control movement.

Advertising is an area where a global standard could enhance the efforts of individual nations to protect public health, by establishing more uniform or basement-level standards around the globe to prevent the tobacco transnationals from exploiting countries with weak legislation or enforcement. The Internet and transboundary satellite transmission of TV ads to countries with TV ad bans require international intervention. World health could benefit from similar international standards on tobacco advertising. Norway and Finland have strict advertising restrictions, and the laws have resulted in a decline in smoking.[3] These laws can be looked to as models in developing domestic and international tobacco control standards.

Another problem that requires international intervention is smuggling. The tobacco transnationals have been implicated in complicity with smuggling of their own cigarettes as a way to establish the brand in new or closed markets, or to avoid taxes. In South Africa, Philip Morris competitor Rembrandt Group filed suit against Philip Morris, accusing the corporation of allowing Marlboro cigarettes to be smuggled into the country.[4] Research demonstrates that smuggling increases along with expansion of the tobacco industry into international markets.[5] In Mexico, smuggled cigarettes account for 30 percent of the market for Marlboro.[6] Shareholder resolutions have been proposed for both Philip Morris and RJR Nabisco in 1998 to establish independent committees to investigate the corporations' roles (direct or indirect) in smuggling their own cigarettes.[7] Duty-free sales, cigarette pricing and taxation, reporting of production and sales, testing and reporting of toxic ingredients, are all areas that require supranational standards and solutions.

There are precedents for such international standards, including the World Health Organization's International Code of Marketing of Breast Milk Substitutes in which INFACT played an active role. The Code was instituted in 1984 as a result of public opposi-

This Marlboro ad on a bank of phone booths in Shanghai, China, has no health warning. INFACT supports efforts to force the US tobacco corporations to abide by US standards where international standards are weaker or nonexistent.[8]

tion to the aggressive marketing and promotion tactics for infant formula by transnational corporations like Nestlé.[9] These promotional tactics resulted in the deaths of approximately one million infants every year, especially in Africa and other economically poor regions.

A resolution was passed at the 10th World Conference on Tobacco or Health in Beijing in August 1997 in support of an International Framework Convention for comprehensive tobacco control.[10] Support from the US and other governments is essential for this to happen. The tobacco corporations are anticipating international action. It is also fiercely opposed and feared by the tobacco industry. News from the Beijing conference about proposals for taking action to combat the "global influence" of the tobacco transnationals prompted this response in an industry trade journal:

> [T]he tobacco industry does have mutual interests around the globe. And, perhaps soon, mutual adversaries too. Maybe it's time for tobacco companies to consider the impossible: balancing commercial interests with a united, coordinated and global front on the industry's behalf.[11]

But public health advocates and concerned citizens around the globe are also uniting to hold accountable these and other transnational corporations that threaten people's lives and the environment.

The tobacco giants have nothing to lose but profits. We have everything to lose: our lives.

NOTES

1   "An International Framework Convention for Tobacco Control," Neil E., Collishaw of the World Health Organization (Presentation at the 10th World Conference on Tobacco or Health), Beijing, Aug., 1997.

2   10th World Conference on Tobacco or Health, Beijing, Aug. 1997.

3   Presentation by Ruth Roemer and Allyn Taylor, World Health Assembly, 10th World Conference on Tobacco or Health, Beijing, Aug. 1997.

4   Raymond Bonner, "Rival Asserts Philip Morris Smuggles in

South Africa," *New York Times,* Nov. 22, 1997.

5   Anthony Flint, "Cigarette Firms Condemn Smuggling, Gain From It," *Boston Globe,* June 10, 1996.

6   "Philip Morris and B.A.T Invest $2B in Mexico," *Tobacco International,* Sept. 1997, p. 9.

7   Interfaith Center on Corporate Responsibility, *The Proxy Resolutions Book,* January 1998, p. 90.

8   Photo provided by Wan-xian Li, MD, Shanghai Medical University, 1997.

9   Doug Johnson, "Confronting Corporate Power: Strategies and Phases of the Nestlé Boycott," *Research in Corporate and Social Performance and Policy,* 1986, p. 323.

10 "Resolutions of the 10th World Conference on Tobacco or Health," Beijing, Aug. 1997.

11 "U.S. Anti's New Approach: Go Global," *Tobacco Reporter,* Oct. 1997, p. 8.

APPENDIX:
Philip Morris and RJR Nabisco Board Members and Corporate Information

Philip Morris Companies, Inc.
120 Park Avenue, New York, NY 10017
212-880-5000

BOARD MEMBERS

Dr. Elizabeth E. Bailey
Professor of Public Policy and Management, University of Pennsylvania; Director, Honeywell

Geoffrey C. Bible
Chair and Chief Executive Officer; Board Member, British Sky Broadcasting

Murray H. Bring
Executive Vice President of External Affairs and General Counsel

Dr. Harold Brown
Counselor, Center for Strategic and International Studies (CSIS), Washington, DC; Partner, Warburg Pincus & Co.

William H. Donaldson
Co-founder and Senior Advisor, Donaldson, Lufkin & Jenrette; Chair, Donaldson Enterprises, Inc.

Jane Evans
President and Chief Operating Officer, Smart TV; Director, Banc One Arizona, Co.; Director, Georgia-Pacific Co.

Robert E.R. Huntley
Retired Counsel to Hunton & Williams

Rupert Murdoch
Chair and Chief Executive Officer of The News Corporation, Limited; Director, MCI Communications; Board Member, British Sky Broadcasting

John D. Nichols
Retired Chair, Illinois Tool Works, Inc.; Director, Rockwell, International Co.

Lucio A. Noto
Chair and CEO, Mobil Oil Corp.

Richard D. Parsons
President, Time Warner, Inc.; Director, Citicorp; Director, Fannie Mae

Roger S. Penske
Chair, Penske Corporation; Chair, Detroit Diesel; Director, General Electric Co.; Director, Gulfstream Aerospace Co.

John S. Reed
Chair and Chief Executive Officer of Citicorp and Citibank, N.A.; Director, Rand Co.; Director, Monsanto Co.

Carlos Slim
Chair, Grupo Carso, S.A. de C.V.; Chair, Teléfonos de México

Stephen M. Wolf
Chair and CEO of US Airways and USAir, Inc.

RJR Nabisco Holdings Corp.
1301 Avenue of the Americas, New York, NY 10019
212-258-5600

BOARD MEMBERS

John T. Chain, Jr.
Former Commander-in-Chief,
Strategic Air Command, USAF;
Former Executive Vice-President,
Safety and Corporate Support,
Burlington Northern RR Co.;
Director, Northrop Grumman Co.

Julius L. Chambers
Chancellor, North Carolina Central
University

John L. Clendenin
Retired CEO; Director, Coca-Cola
Enterprises, Inc.; Director, Home
Depot, Inc.; Director, Wachovia
Co.; Director, Kroger Co.

Steven F. Goldstone
Chair, President, General Counsel
and Chief Executive Officer

Ray J. Groves
Retired Chair and Chief Executive
Officer, Ernst & Young; Director,
Electronic Data Systems Co.

L. Dennis Kozlowski
Chair, President and Chief Executive Officer, Tyco International
Ltd.; Director, Raytheon Co.;
Director, Thiokol Co.

H. Eugene Lockhart
President, BankAmerica
Corporation's Global Retail Bank

Theodore E. Martin
Chief Executive Officer, Barnes
Group

John G. Medlin, Jr.
Chair, Wachovia Corporation and
Wachovia International Banking;
Director, USAir, Inc.; Director,
BellSouth Co.

Rozanne L. Ridgway
Former US Assistant Secretary of
State and Co-chair of the Atlantic
Council of the United States; Chair,
Baltic American Enterprise
Foundation; Director, Citibank;
Director, Boeing Co.; Director,
Union Carbide Co.; Director, Sara
Lee Co.; Director, Minnesota
Mining and Manufacturing Co.

DON'T BUY IT!

JOIN INFACT'S TOBACCO INDUSTRY BOYCOTT AND SEND A MESSAGE TO PHILIP MORRIS AND RJR NABISCO:

To: Geoffrey Bible, *Chief Executive Officer, Philip Morris Companies, Inc.*
Steven Goldstone, *Chief Executive Officer, RJR Nabisco, Inc.*

Dear Mr. Bible and Mr. Goldstone,

As chief executives of the two largest US-based tobacco corporations, you know that tobacco use kills three million people worldwide each year, and that 60% of smokers start before they're even 14 years old. You also know that Philip Morris' Marlboro is the world's #1 cigarette brand in the US, and that smoking rates among young women rose substantially after Philip Morris introduced Virginia Slims. RJR Nabisco's Joe Camel promotional campaign was incredibly successful at recruiting youth to smoke, and even with the withdrawal of this advertising scheme from the US, youth are still being bombarded with Joe Camel and new marketing techniques worldwide. Your corporations have used political influence over the US government to force open international markets and expand this preventable epidemic.

I am joining INFACT's focused Campaign on Philip Morris and RJR Nabisco, calling on you and the rest of the tobacco industry to:

Stop marketing and promotion that appeals to children and young people;
Stop spreading tobacco addiction internationally;
Stop influence over and interference in public health policy;
Stop deceiving people about the dangers of tobacco;
Pay the high costs of health care associated with the tobacco epidemic.

continued

I pledge to participate in INFACT's international boycott of Philip Morris and RJR Nabisco products until you stop your abusive practices.

NAME	ADDRESS	CITY/STATE/COUNTRY
1.		
2.		
3.		
4.		
5.		
6.		
7.		
8.		
9.		
10.		

Please Return to:
> **INFACT**
> **256 Hanover Street**
> **Boston, MA 02113 USA**
> **(617) 742-4583**

ADDITIONAL THANKS

Additional thanks to the following INFACTers—together you sustain our campaigning and our organization:

CAP (Corporate Abuse Prevention) Team Members

D. & L. Adams
A. Adelson
J. Alexander
S. Andersen
R. & A. Anderson
A. Andrews
K. Andrews
B. Archibald
N. Aucella
J. Bach
G. Baines
R. & D. Bancroft
S. Beecher
E. & M. Bender
B. Berg
S. & F. Beville
D. Bloch
T. Boutell & M. Grant
D. Bowers
F. Broadhurst
H. Brody
T. Brown
L.H. Buada
K. Buzan
M. Calen
W. Call & A. Falsafi
H.O. Campbell
K. & R. McDonald, Carondelet Community
E. & D. Carroll
M. Casey
A. Chaney
J. Chaplick
J. Chapman
Z. & L. Charles
T. & N. Chase
J. Christie
S. & R. Citta
G. Clark
K. Clawson
J. Costanza
W. Craig
K. Cross
L. De Sitter
M. Dopkins
J. & L. Doyle
N. Dragutinovic
B.A. Drew

L. Dustrude
D. Ecoffey
J.B. Farrell
R. & J. Fassett
W. Fassett & K. Mahony
J. Feit
P. Fiege
D. Fine
C. Fletcher
A. Floyd
C. Folger
C.B. Foster
E.W. French
J. & J. Friedman
J. Gelbspan
R. & A. Gelbspan
T. Gelbspan
M. & V. Gerritsen
D. Goldman
J. & G. Good
M. Greene
R. & G. Gutierrez
W.D. Hall
J.S. Hamner
R. & S. Harding
J. Hart
T. & C. Hartman
C.S. Haven
J. Hayden
S. Heenan
D.W. Hendon
F. & M.A. Herbert
C. & H. Hicks
G. Ho
H. Hoffman
J. & T. Horan
M. & V. Hyvarinen
D. James
C. & M. Johnson
K. Johnson
A.B. Johnston
R. Kahn
E. Katz
P. & M. Keating
D. & K. Kelly
R.M. Kevess
E. Kimble
W. & J. King
E.M. Kleinhans
S. Kline
M. Koren

B. Krauss-Christensen
J. Kussamaul
E. Lamy
S. Lasalle
L. Lawler
P. Layden
S. Leeds &. D. Bruni
M. Leonardini
S. & H. Levine
D. Levins
D. Lewis
S. Lieblein
O. & F. Loud
M. Lovelace & D. Fagaly
J. & T. Lowry
T. Lynch
A. J. Macdonald
D. M. Magruder
C. Malecka
M. Malone
E. K. Martinez
O. S. Mason
J. & S. McAlpine
L. McCall
M. McCue
B. McMurray
A. Merrick
D. M. Milburn
M. P. & M. L. Miller
J. & B. Mogulescu
O. Moon
B. Morse, Jr.
E. Moseley
D. & N. Mulvey
N. J. Newcomb
J. Olmstead
C. & E. O'Shea
M. Padilla
S. & S. Pearl
P. & R. Peckham
J. Petkus
E. Pettersen
G. & K. Price
L. & B. Pryor
T. Re
M. Reedy
D. Renick
J. & J. Rissman
A.E. Rosati
B. Rottger
M. Roush

H. & S. Royaltey
E. & A. Rudin
C. S. Rusk
M.A. Ryan
E. Schaeffer
B. Schenck
M. Schultz & J. Raymond
S. Shoresman
D. L. Smith
K. Smith
L. Smith
C. & G. Sova
H. B. Strader
J. K. Swanson
A.C. Swift
C.L. Tebbetts
E. Thompson
M.G. Thornton
L. Tuchler
J.C. Turner
J.J. Underhill
R. Ungar
J. & C. Upshaw
A. Uttich
J. Van Fleet
A. Wakefield
P. Walker
K. Weihs
C. Welch
W.T. Wheeler
E.B. Winters
B. Withrow
K.H. Wolff
F. Wood
E. & J. Yackel
M. Zant
J. & F. Zilka

INFACT Supporters

B. Aaron
D. & M. Aaron
F.E. Abbey
F.P. Abrams
E.H. Abts
B.L. Adams
E.L. Adams
F. Adams & S. McCafferty
H. & M. Adams
J.A. Adams

R. Adams
T. Adcock
L. Adelson
Adrian Dominican
    Sisters
Adorers of the Blood of
    Christ
W. J. Aebersold
M. Agresti
E. & I. Aikin
D.M. Aland
D.W. Albert
C. Albeston
A. & G. Albrecht
J. J. Alder
H. J. Alfini
A. & S. Alland
V. Allard
E.H. Allen, Jr.
E.W. Allen
G.C. Allen
H. V. Allen
S. Allen
T. C. Allen
W. & J. Alles
J. & D. Alley
J. & V. Allison
M.R. Alper
R. Alpert
M.B. Alworth
J. Amory
C.E. Andersen
D. Andersen
Hugh J. Andersen
    Foundation
C. Anderson
C.F.W. Anderson
G.E. Anderson, Jr.
I. & B. Anderson
J.W. Anderson
M. Anderson
R.D. Anderson
R.E. Anderson
R.W. Anderson
S. Anderson
S.A. Anderson
T. Anderson
M. Andrews
S.B. Andrus
F. Anglin
R.E. Anthony
T. Apley
J.L. Appleton
M. Archenhold
M. Arden
S. Arent & B. Wolfman
M. Arguelles
F. Arkin
B.J. Armstrong
F.A. Armstrong
L.W. Armstrong
R.E. Arndal
W. Arndt
J. Arnold
J.G. Arnold
C. & J. Arnquist

D.C. Arntson
A. Aronoff
J.H. Arwood
A. Ash
M. Atkins
H. Atkinson
T. Atkinson
Atlantic City Area
    Friends
D. Austin
A. & S. Babad
R. Bach & L. Parrish-
    Bach
K.D. Bachman
H.H. Bacon
C.A. Bade
G. Baehr
A. & M. Bagaason
R. Bagga
S.B. Bagley
C.Bailey
J. Baime
B. Bair
H. & L. Baker
K.G. Baker
L. Baker
W. Baker
E. & G. Baker-Smith
A. Baldwin
F. & B. Baldwin
V. Balester
L. & M. Balint
J. & D. Ball
S. & B. Ball
Benedictine Sisters of
    Baltimore
D.P. Baltzer
F.B. Bancroft
L.M. Barber
M. Barbieri
M. Bardelson
D. Barham
E.H. Barker
E. Barlow
S. Barnard
L. Baron
M.R. Barral
W.F. Barrett
S. Barry
R. & J. Barsanti
C.A. Barsanti
L.H. Barstow
G. Bason
G.M. Bastien
P. & R. Baty
H. & H. Bauer
R. Bauer
L.S. Bauers
A.W. Baumann, Jr.
E. Baumgartner
S. Bayer
L. Beaky
A. W. & D.K. Beam
G. Bean
J. & B. Beatty
R. & C.Beauchamp

F. & E. Beck
J. Beck
M. Becker
R. Becker
G.F. Bedding
P. Beetle
A.T. Behrmann
J.S. Beigler
B. Beineke
A. & D. Belansky
D. Bell
N.J. Bell
V.H. Bell
W. Bell
R. & J. Bellavance
M. Bellin
A. Bemko
G.L. Bender
H. Bender
R. Bender
V. Bengal
B. Benson
W. Benz
M. Berg
G. Berger
J.M. Berger
C. Bergmann
E. Berke
P. Berkery
K. Berkson
S. & V. Berman
S. Berner
G. Bernett
J. Bernhard
E. Bernhardt
M. & F. Bernhardt
H. & D. Bernstein
M. Bernstein
R.H. Bernstein
M. & E. Berrie
J. Berrigan
R.J. & J.L. Berry
W. Bertsch
S. & C. Bettison-Sher
E. Betzig
J.R. Beveridge
J. & A. Bezila
G. Bible
K. Bible
D. Bibus
A. & J. Bice
J. Bierman
C. Bigler
A. Bilik
G. Bill
S.C. Billenness & B.
    Passoff
D. & G.J. Billmeier, Jr.
J. Birke
D. Birnbaum
P. Birnie
J. Bjork
H. & S. Black
R.L. & H.C. Black
R.H. Blanding
S. & H. Blankenhorn

C.A. Bleistein
M. Bletterman
S. & R. Blickensderfer
R. & M.B. Blinn
B. Bloch
S. Bloch
A. Block
F. Blom
G. Blombach
D. Blue
J. J. Blum
J.K. Blume & M.
    Burnley Blume
M.W. Blumenthal
D. Blumner
A. Bobrick
C. Bock
R. & F. Boehm
H. Bogotch
C. Bohnn
M. Boime
T. Boisseau & K.
    Hoppe
E.D. Boldt
J.L. Boling
R. Bolman
G. Bond
R. Bondurant
S. J.Bongle
R. & A. Booth
B. Crosby Booth &
    T.W. Booth
R.B. Borovec
B. Bossie
C. & P. Bouwman
C. Bowen
J.F. Bowen
J.L. Bowen
N.W. Bowker
P.J. Bowlby
M. Bowman
J. Bream
E. Breilid
H.A. Breininger
J. Brengelman
M. Brennan
L. Brenner
M. Breslow
D. Bresnick
A. Bretz
B. Bretz
R.W. Brewer
G. Brewton
A. & K. Bricker
C.H. Bright
W. & G. Brinker
L.P. Brinton
B. Britain
C. Broadwell
H. Brockaman
M.L. Brodie
B. Brodsky
M. & L. Brody
J.C. Bronars Jr.
J. Brooker
G. & J. Brookman

J. Brooks
S. Brower
D. & M. Brown
F.S. Brown
H. Brown
J. Brown
K. Brown
L. Brown
L. & E. Brown
M. Brown
N. Brown
O. & J. Brown
R. Brown
W. & S. Brown
R. Browne & L. Katon
S. Browne
N. Broyles
E. Bruck
L. Bruckmann
D. Brutus
P. & J. Bryan
L. & B. Bryner
I. & M. Buchin
A. Buchman
H. & E. Buck
E.F. Buckley
J. Buckley
F. & J.H. Buckner
C. F. & J. Buechner
B.A. Buehler
P. Buendia
J.A. & A.B. Bueti
J. & S. Buhr
K.M. Bullitt
A. Bundy
D. & E. Bunting
G. & V. Burchell
A. & R. Burckhardt
J. Burke
G. Burlingham
C. Burnley
E.S. Burns
T. & D. Burns
D. Burnstein & J. Borck
D. & L. Burtis
L. Burtzloff
S. Bushman
C. Buswell
E. & G. Butcher
P. Butler
T. Butler
J. Butters
M. Butterworth
T. Butterworth
S. & J. Bykofsky
E. Caffrey
T. Caffrey & J. Vroom
L. Caine
D. & M. Caldwell
H. Callback & L. Aldrich
D. & C. Calleri
M.M. Calodney
G. Campagna
M. Campbell

D. & C. Campbell
J. & N. Campbell
E. Campuzano
H.R. Canada
B. Candee
C. Candell
J. Cann
R. Cann
D. & M. Cantor Paster
I. Cantos
E. Capelle
G. Caplan
E. Capone
G. & P. Carbone & K. Malone
Y. & J. Carl
J. Carley
J.A. Carley
F. Carlin
J. & G. Carman
N.H. Carman
R. & L. Carman
J. & E. Carney
J.B. Caron
B. Carpenter
D. Carr
R.E. Carr
W. & M.Carry
M.E. Carson
R.L. Carter
U. Casanova
R. Case
L. Casler
A. & N. Casper
M. & N. Casper
B.I. Castleman
S. Castleman
Catholic Diocese of Richmond
Catholics for Justice
D. Cattell
J.F. Caul
C.& S. Caulson
L.F. Cavalieri
B. & R. Cavin
W. & C. Ceglowski
G. Celente
D. Ceremello
C. Ceronsky
M. Cerqueira
S. Chacker & J.C.Bourrut
S.J. Chacker
L.W. Chafe
B. & C. Chalmer
R.P. Chamberlain
G. Chambon
C. & L. Chandler
B. Chantland
G. & A. Chapman
K. Chase
T. Chase
S. Chasinov
D.N. Cheifetz
P. Cherner
H. Chesler

B.G. & M. Chieffo
H. Chikowski
W. & N. Child
M.Tyler Childress
E. Childs-Gowell
B. Chipouras
A. Chitouras
J.R. Chitwood
A.L. Christensen
C. & D. Christensen
M.J. Christian
E.S. Chwast
E. Ciaccio & V. Loudis
D. Clapp
D.W. Clark
F. & W. Clark
I. Clark
J. & D. Clark
K.S. Clark
L. Clark
R. & B. Clark
H. & M. Clarke
M.D. Clarke
A. Clayton
W.J. Clayton
T. Cleary
M. Cleeton
D.S. Cleland
A. Clement
P. Clifford & P. Mullins
H. Clinebell
D. & A. Clinton
R. & F. Clinton
L.K. Clorfene-Casten
V.L. Close
J.M. Cluett
P. Clyons
E. Cobb
S. & D. Cobin
D. Cochran
M.B. Cochran
D. & K. Cochrane
W. Cogswell
A. Cohen
B. Cohen
C.L. Cohen
G. Cohen
H. & N. Cohen
H.J. Cohen
J. Cohen
M. Cohen
R. & C. Cohen
V. Cohen
E. Cohen-Cole
M.M. Cohn
L. Colby
N. Cole & C. Brady
R.J. Coleman
K. & T.Colescott
E.C & N. Collias
J. H. Collier
R.W. & F. Collier
C. Colt & K. Donnelly
M.T. Coltharp
R. Compton
R. Conatser

R.S. Condon
B. & J. Congdon
B. Conger
R.D. Conklin
R. Conn
S. & M.L. Conna
J.J. Connolly
R.M. Connolly
A.G. Cook
N.G. Cook
C. Coombs
W. Coombs
P. Copeland
F.G. Copetas
S. Corcoran
B. Corr
G. & F. Corum
J. & C. Corum
E. Corwin
S. & R. Cory
J. & T. Coskey
H. & B. Cottle
M. Cottrill
M.M. Courant
G.K. Cousins
M. Cowley
F.V. Cowling & P.R. Dorn
E.M. Craig
F. & M. Craig
M. Craig
M.E. Craig
D.H. Brooks & S. Cramer
L. Cranberg
C. Crane
M.M. Crosthwaite
D. Crowell
P. Crowley
M. Crusius & T. Lent
R. Csarny
F.P. Culleton
R. & K. Culpepper
J. K. Cummings
R. Curci
S. Curley
M.R. Curtis
D. Cutler
S. Cutler & J. Stuart
K. & H. Dahmen
M. Daitz
S. Dale
Dallas Peace Center
G. J. Dalzell
K. Danaher
B. Dancis
P. Daniel
H. Danielowitz
S. Daniels
W. & E. Daniels
E.M.K. Darby
L. Darga
A. J. Dasburg
C. Dauber
J. Dauer
A. & C. Daughters

J.D. Freeman
L. Freeman
J. & L. Freilich
F. & A. Frellick
D. French & K. Greeley
W. French
D.C. Frey
C. Fried
M.D. Fried
D.L Friedman
F. & J. Friedman
J. Friedman
N.M. Friedman
S. Friedman
D.J. Froba
B. & M. Frost
J.R. Froyd
A. & S. Fry
C.E. Fry
L.L. Fuchs
E. Fuerst
G.S. Fuller
G. Fulmer
I. Funk
J. Furniss
A. Fusco
D. Fusco
E. Gaestel
P. & J. Gaffney
A.F. Gagne
J. Gaines
F. Galea
K. & M. Galewyrick
J. Gallant
A.F. Gallistel
J. Galloway
F. & M. Galluccio
R. & L.Galt
W.P. Gambert
S.F. Gambescia
R. Garavel
F. Gardner
A.P. Gardner
E. Garmire
B. Garrett
D. Garrett
A. Garrison
W.P. Garton
D. Garvey
G. Garwood
G. Gasser
D. & T. Gay
M.A. Gebhart
W.M. Gegg
F. Geiger
A.M. Geisler
J. & T. Gelder
M. Gelder & M. R. Luecke
R. Geller
R.C. Gelsey
D.B. Genung
L. & J. Gerber
R.P. Gerhardstein
T. Gerlits

H.Gerritsen
J. & B. Gerstein
L.A. Gervase
J.M. Gessell
N. & A. Geyer
V.H. Gibson
D. Giese
M.M. Giese
H. & D. Giessler
J.H. Gignoux
M. Gilbert
N. Gilden
M.E. Gillespie
J. Gilmore
J. & L. Gingerich
R.A. Ginsburg
A.D. & R. Giovanella
A. & S. Girard
D.L. Gittes
S. & V. Glasband
J.P & B. Glass
A.J. Glasser
S. Glassner
P. Glenn
B. Glick-Rieman
M. Glicksman
Global Peace Foundation
T. Gloster
F.W. Glover
S. Gluck
C. Goan
C. Goetz
T. Goetze
I. & A. Goldreyer
E.D. Goldsmith
P. Goldsmith
G. Goldstein
G.R. Goldstein
H. Goldstein
D. & R. Golfen
P. & R. Golombek
L. & E. Good
The Good Works Foundation
D. Goodman
J. Goodman
R.W. Goodman
W. Goodman
A.M. Goodrich
J. Bell & R. Goodwin
D. Goodwin
N. Goodwin
S. Goodwin
E. & R. Gorden
G. & E. Gordon
J. Gordon
M.A. Gordon
D. Gottsegen
M.A. Govednik
R. Graap
J. Grabowski
P. Grace
E.S. Graefe
J.H. Graham
M.G. Graham

J.B. Grant
R.G. Grant
D.B. Gras
F.A. Graves
D.M. Graybeal
A.M. Grayson
E. & C. Greb
B. Green
G. Green
R.G. Green
J. Green-Walker
B. Greenbaum
D. Greenberg
H. & M. Greenberg
J. Greenberg
D. Greene
G. Greene
S. Greene
L. & D. Greenfield
E.M. Greenhill
P. Greenman
C. Greenwood
M. Gregg
J. Gregoli
J. Gregory
L. & B. Grendahl
M. & J. Griffin
E. Griswold
R.B. Grooters
W.E. Grose
J. Grossholtz
M. Grossman
L. Grout
R. Gruenberg
T. Grunewald
D.S. Grutman
P.S. Guillen
I. Gullen
J. F. Gummer
C. Gundlach
J. & M. Gurewitz
F. & K. Gusz
J.B. Guthrie
J. Gutstadt
M.S. Gyr
H. & L. Haacke
F.W. Haase
A.C. Hackman
L. Hadac
C.D. Haddad
S.K. Haddad
C. & R. Hadley
F. Hagan
M. Hagenberger
S.L. Haines
S. Halebsky
A. Hall
D.C. Hall
D.G. Hall
D.W. Hall
E.F. Hall
T. Hallahan
R. & W. Hallinan
I. Halsted
R. Hamburger
V. Hamill

D. Hamilton
L. Hamilton
P.F. Hamilton
L. & E. Hammer
R. Handewith
D.S. Handwerker
E.R. Hankin
C. Hannibal
H. Hannum
L.C. Hansen
W.A. Hansen
J. Hanson
K. Hanson
V. Hanson
B. Hardy
M. & C. Hargiss
M.C. Harms
G. & J. Harper
L.F. Harper
K. Harrell
J. & D. Harrington
A. Harris
J.L. Harris
M.R. Harris
R. Harris
V.L. Harris
H. Harrison
E. Harsch
R. Harstad
B. Hart
E. Hart
D. & G. Harter
S. & T. Harter
C. Hartman
S. Hartman
R.J. Hartmann
E. Hartsoe & R. Katz
D. & J. Hartsough
P. & K. Hartzman
B. & M. Harvey
G. Hasen
I.O. Hassel
K. Hasson
A. & J. Hastings Lovejoy
F.B. Hatch
J.V. Hatch
M. Hathaway
R. Haugh
T. Haughton
M. Hausman
R. & E. Hausman
V.W. Havens
M. Hayes
C. Hayman
J.F. & M.S. Hayward
M.C. Hazard
M. & J. Heald
S. Hedrick
R. Heepe
D.M. Heffernon
J.S. Hege
I. & S. Hegg
D. & E. Heidtmann
K. & H. Heikel
J. Heiko

M. Kirscheimer
C. Kittle
B.O. Kjelshus
M. Klas
J. Klecka
H. & D. Klein
R. & C. Klein
M. Klemm
I. Klevens
C. Kleymeyer
E. & E. Klibaner
L. Klingeman
B. Klopott
E. Kloppe
R. & L. Kloss
C. & B. Klosterman
G. & F. Knechtges
N. & M. Knoblauch
R. Knobler
J. Knowles
R. Kobayashi
S. Kober- Zeller
N. Koch
A. Kochman
U. Koester
E. & E. Koether
W. Kohn
P. & L. Kolasinski
P. & T. Kolojeski
S. Konopka
J. Kontrimas
G. Koons
N. Koponen
O. Koppell
G. & B. Korn
M. Kornbluth
P. Kovac
P. Kowal
R. Kozak
E. Kraft
F. & S. Kraft
K. Kram
G. & A. Krasner
P. Kratz
D. Krehbiel
V. Krejcie
F. & J. Kremer
B. Krieger
D. Kandel
H. & C. Kroll
W. Krueger
D. Krull
B. & S. Kublin
N. & A. Kukulan
L. Kummer
M. Kunkel
R. Kunreuther
A. Kushner
R. & R. La Monica
S. Laby
H. Ladd
M. Ladd
M. Laituri
L. and E. Lake
J. Lamar
W. Lambert

J.T. Lambie
R. Lammers
S. Lampert
M. Lamy
H. Lander
J. Landes
J. Landkamer
J. Landles
H. Lando
D. Landy
B. Lane
M. Lane
S. & P. Lang
B. Langan
L. Langer, Jr.
B. & J. Lapham
C. Lapine
P. Lappala
D. Larco
L. & K. Larson
D. & M. Lathrop
B. Latner
R. Laurie
J. & J. Lavely
A.& E. Lawrence
L. Lawrence
H. Lebowitz
B.& P. Ledbetter
B.& R. Leeds
C. Leeman
E. Leeper
R.& M. Leeson
C. & A. Lefevre
M. & G. Lefstein
A.& S. Legg
J.G. Legg
C. Leibowitz
M. & N. Leiserowitz
R. & A. Lemon
P. L. Lent
M. Leonard
P. & J. Lersch
J. & T. Leuba
S. Leventhal
E.G. Levi
H. & B. Levie
E. Levine
A. Levine
M. Levine
P. Levis
C. Levison
A. & P. Levy
S. Levy
C. Lewis
D.M. Lewis
D.R. Lewis
F.E. Lewis
J. & F. Lewis
J. & G. Lewis
K. Lewis
J.M. Lichtenstein
O. & E. Liddell
D. Lieb
E.J. Lieberman
J. Liebowitz
L. Liederman

C. Lilley
B. & L. Lincoln
K. Lind
L. Lind
E. Lindblom
W. Lindley
J. Lineweaver
D. & S. Linney
H. Linsmayer
M.C. Lipkin
R. Lipkis
L. Lippard
I.A. Lippman
M.J. Lippman
A.K. Lipton
M. Lipton
Little Franciscans of
   Mary
C. Lloyd
G. Lloyd
J. & J. Lloyd
R. Lloyd
N. Lob
A. Lobel
H. Lobel
J. & G. Lobenstine
F. & C. Locke
G. & A. Locker
R. Lockhart
A. Locklear
C. Loe
L. Loe
Y. Logan
L. Lohr
S. Londe
L. Longo
B. & J. Lonneman
H. Lord
S. Loria
K. Loring
M. Loring
M. Louaillier
T. Lourbacos
A. & E. Lovejoy
N. Lovejoy
J. Lovelace
M. Lovette
P. Lowe
R. Lowenherz
M. Lowy
E. Lubbers
S. & R. Lubow
F. Lucido
R. Luckmann
H. Ludwig
R. Luecke
E. Lugo
M. Lukens
M. Lulucki
H. Luther
J. Lutschg
L. Lyman
C. Lynch
E. & C. Lynd
H. Lynn
J. Lynn

R. Lynn
H. Lyon
R. Lyons
A. & B. Mabbs
G. Mabus
B. Maccoll
W. & J. Macdonald
F. Mack
R. & S. Mack
S. Mack
I. Mackintosh
M. Maclay
E. Macnichol
E. & S. Macy
K. Madden
E. Maderios
M. Madias
J. Madison
T. Mager
S. Magill
J. Maguire
J. Maher & E.
   Sankisian
R. & P. Malchow
W. Malloy
K. & P. Man
D. Mancini
D. Mann
I. Mann
J. Mannix
T. Mantel
M. Manwell
N. Marcus
C. Marion
B. Mark
C. Marks
A. Marlatt
B. Marquardson
N. Marquez
A. Marsak
T. Marsh
D. Marshall
G. Marshall
J. Marshall
E. Martin
I. Martin
J. Martin
R. Martin
L. Martineau
M. Martinez
W. Martinson
O. Mason
M. Massar
F. & N. Mather
M. Matheson
D. & J. Mathison
B. Mathon
I. Matisse
D. & S. Matteson
C. Matthews
A. Mattuck
T. Maul
W. Maxfield
E. Maxwell
C. Mayer
O. & H. Mayer

S. Orlow
H. Orndorff
E. & C. Orr
R. Orsi
W. Osborn
I. Osborne
M. Osborne
K. Oser
H. & S. Oshrain
S. Oskamp
S. Osofsky
R. Ossont
E. & R. Ostrow
L. Oswald
C. Otis
Our Lady of Victory
   Missionary Sisters
M. Overs
E. Owens
E. Oxfeld
J. Paape
D. & K. Pack
J. Paden
J. Pagano-Cragnolin
B. Page
J. Page
T. Page
W. Palich
G. & E. Palm
J. Palms & D. Petty
J. Panchot
J. & S. A. Panci
M. Panzer
J. & D. Papp
G. Pardal
R. & E. Parker
F. Parkman, Jr.
W. Parry
H. W. & M. L. Parson
M. A. Pasternack
P. Pasterz
B. Patterson
D. A. Paulsen
A. Paulson
A. Paxton
P. Peach
E. C. Peara
R. Pearl
J. A. Pearlman
D. & L. Pearson
D. & D. Pearson
G. Pearson
J. M. Pearson
M. Pearson
N. Peattie
J. S. Peden
R. & R. Peeples
L. Peisson
H. A. Pellett
L. Peltz
D. & E. Pelz
K. Pence
L. C. Penniman
M. E. Pennock
M. Peratis
S. A. Perez

C. Perisho
J. Perkins
B. Perlman
M. & D. Perlman
E. Perrin
F. E. Perry
J. Perry
R. Perry
F. Persons
F. Pestana
A. & B. Peters
M. Peters
L. Peterson
B. Petroff
K. E. Petron
D. Pettengill
T. & D. Pettes
W. W. Pettus
J. Petty
B. Pfau
B. Phillips
D. Phillips
J. D. Phillips
M. B. Phillips
J. & T. Pickell
R. J. Pierce
S. Pierce
T. Pierce
C. & C. Pieterman
E. & B. Pillar
C. Pillsbury
K. Pillsbury & C.
   Marshall
M. Pimsler
D. F. Plocher
L. A. Plumlee
E. Plunkett
M. Polimeni
S. Polishuk
A. & D. Pollitt
B. K. Pomerantz
J. Pomerantz
R. & J. Weed
   Pomerantz
D. M. Pomeroy
C. N. Pond
G. Pope
M. Pope
A. V. Porter
W. E. Porter
E. Posel
C. & M. Pottle
A. P. Poulson
P. Powdermaker
H. Powell
W. & M. A. Powell
M. Powers
J.F. Pratt
R. Pregulman
H. Prensky
D. G. Presley
A. Price
B. Price
J. & S. Price
M. Prichard
A. Priddy

M. & D. Priest
A. Prigoff
E. H. Primoff
H. D. Prince
S. Pritchard
B. & C. Prokop
E. Puckett
M. L. & J. Puibell
L. D. & K. Putney
F. Quartarone
D. L. Quinn
R. H. Rachals
Racine Dominican
   Sisters
R. Rafn
T. Raihl
J. Rainwater
H. Raizen
M. Ralph
P. & R. Ralph
M. J. Ramaekers
D.D. Randall
A. & J. Randles
S. Ranish
K. Raphael
W. Ratzlaff
S. Ratzmann
D. J. Raver
M. J. Ravnitzky
K. & E. Rawson
P. Raymond
R. & J. Raymond
C. A. Reamer
D. & E. Reardon
R. Rechnitz
R. Redfern
F. Reed
M.H. Reed
E. J. Rees
R. Rees
K. H. Reese
E. Regan
K. Reich
R. S. Reich
D. M. Reichardt
D. Reid
J. M. Reid
J. R. & F. Reid
J. H. Reiff
J. L. Reindl
K. Reiner
N. Reisner
S. Reiter
H. Relin
D. Relis
M. L. Reno
M. & F. Renstrom
V. Reuther
E. M. & J. E. Reynolds
K. Reynolds
L. Reynolds
P. Reynolds
R. L. Reynolds
L. Rezeau
M. Rhodes
M. Rhys

Q. Ribordy
D. T. & R. M. Rice
K. Rich
S. Rich
H. Richard
B. Richards
J. Richards
S. & W. Richards
B. H. Richardson
M. B. Richardson
R. E. Richardson
C. & S. Richmond
M. Richter
T. & D. Richter
M. Rickard
G. M. Ricker
J. & P. Riebel
J. Rigg
R. L. Rigg
J. Righthand
P. A. Rindler
E. J. Rinkel
A. M. Rivera
I. E. Roaheim
D. & S. Roak
G. L. Robb
H. E. Robb
H. Robbins
J. D. Robbins
N. J. Roberge
E. Roberson
C. & C. Roberts
E. B. Roberts
G. & J. Roberts
H. D. & C. G. Roberts
J. Roberts
M. Roberts
N. Roberts
M. Robertson
M. Robertson
A. Robin
E. Robins
J. Robinson
K. J. Robinson
R. Robinson
S. C. Robinson
R. & J. Roby
T. & M. Roby
R. A. Rock
W. J. Rockler
D. Rockwell
B. L. Rockwood
J. J. Rodell
R. & J. Rodewald
B. Z. Rofkar
C. & L. Rogers
E. & V. Rogers
P. Rogers
H. Rohr
J. J. & K. Rok
D. Romeo
R. E. Ronsheim
R. D. Roode
D. Rose
J. A. Rose
S. R. Rose

J. Roseman
B. & S. Rosen
E. Rosenberg
H. W. Rosenberg
S. & R. Rosenberg
W. F. Rosenblatt
H. V. Rosenthal
J. Rosenthal
D. S. Rosenwald
S. & J. Rosner
F. J. Ross
J. M. Ross
M. L. S. Ross
I. Rossey
F. Roth
J. C. Roth
M. M. Roth
J. Rothman
W. Rouse
E. & E. Rowland
D. Rubenstein
B. Rubin
S. Rubin
B. & A. Ruckman
D. Ruckman
J. Rudel
E. & A. Rudin
J. & A. Rudnick
A. Rudovsky-Cornfeld
D. P. Ruehl
R. & A. Ruffner
W. & S. Rupel
M. B. Russell
N. Russell
R. & J. Russell
R.H. Russell
W. & B. Russell
J. & B. Rutledge
E. Ryan
A. J. Ryland
J. Saemann
S. Saile
C. & E. Saling
L. Sally
J. Salmon
R. Saltman
M.G. Salvadori
M. Salzer
G. Salzman
P. Samples
V. Samter
D. Samuelson
H. & B. Sanborn
J. & B. Sanders
M. Sanderson-Bolanos
B. Sandlin
B. Sandri
S. & R. Sapon
D. Sarason
J. Sargent & L. Blair
A. Sarinana
C. B. Sartor
D. & J. Sauer
W. Sauey
S. Saulvester
C. A. Saunders

R. Sauser
A. E. Savage
R. & M. A. Savard
E. & J. Savery
T. F. Saxby
R. Saxe
L. Sayre
J. & J. Scaglione
C. Schachet & N. Rusk
R. & A. Schacht
E. Schaeffer
P. & E. Schaefer
P. Schakel
J. Schalch
G. Schartle
E. Schatz
A. Schaupp
D. C. Scheer
D. & S. Scheinfeld
G. & C. Scheldorf
G. Schiff & M. Cohen
B.E. Schilling
J. Schindler
B. D. Schlesinger
D. & H. Schlesinger
E. D. Schley
E. & M. Schlinger
L. Schlosberg
S. A. Schmitt
J. Schmitz
S. Schnapp
H. H. Schnautz
D. Schneider
F. Schneider
M. Schneider
M. Schneider
S. R. Schnur
N. Schoellkopf
T. Schoenbaum
N. & R. Schoenke
K. Schoman
School Sisters of Notre
    Dame
D. & J. Schramm
J. L. Schrock
L. Schroeter
B. & J. Schubert
J. Schumaker
H. Schut
D. Schwab
B. E. Schwartz
E. Schwartz
M. Schwartz
J. Schweitzer
C. & H. R Schwyzer
B. & M. Scott
F. G. Scott
I. & D. Scott
J. Scott
S. T. Scott
N. Scrivens
A. Seabrook
G. Seagert
G. Seaman
C. E. Sears
B. & F. Seasholes

L. & Mrs. Seaver
K. Segal
D. Segaloff
W. S. Selig
E. & P. Te Selle
S. Senet
I. Senn
F. Senska
O. Senz
J. & Y. Sexton
D. & M. Shainin
A. Shalit
A. & M. Shank
M. M. Shanley
H. Shapiro
L. G. Shapiro
M. Shapiro
R. Shapiro
N. L. Sharfman
J. Shaw
M. J. Shaw
C. M. Sheap
R. & K. Shearer
J. Sheldon
S. P. Sheldon
E. Shellenberger
A. Shelton
W. Shen
C. Shepard & D.
    Moritz
M. & R. Shepard
P. & B. Shepherd
S. Shepherd
E. Sherberg
B. Sherman
J. Sherman
A. Sherry
R. Sheviakov
J. J. Shields
C. & E. Shimeall
S. W. Shimer
M. Shinkle
E. & B. Shneyer
B. & W. Shockley
C. Shoemaker
L. Shooman
Mr. & Mrs. W. Shostal
J. & J. Shott
R. Shoul
G. & E. Shoun
B. Shouse
B. Shubin
H. L. Shuken
R. Shultz
W. L. Shuman
R. Shy & K. Zamarin
P. & D. J. Sickles
D. P. Sidebotham
M. Siebielec
D. Sieck
S. R. Siege
A. Siegel
R. & A. Siegfried
P. & D. Siliciano
J. C. Sill
W. & O. Silna

J. C. Silver
S. & K. Silverman
J. Silverstein
J. & S. Silverstein
H. Stevenson Simmons
E. Simon
G. Simon
C. Simpson
P. Simpson
P. & L. Simpson
D. W. Sims
Sisters of Charity
Sisters of Charity
    Center
Sisters of Charity,
    Incarnate Word
Sisters of Charity,
    Leavenworth
Sisters of Charity of
    Nazareth
Sisters of Charity, St.
    Augustine
Sisters of Divine
    Providence
Sisters of the Good
    Shepherd
Sisters of the Holy
    Cross
Sisters of the Holy
    Family of Nazareth
Sisters of Mercy of St.
    Louis
Sisters of Providence
Sisters, Servants of the
    Immaculate Heart
Sisters of St. Dominic
Sisters of St. Francis,
    Oldenburg
Sisters of St. Francis,
    Philadelphia
Sisters of St. Joseph
Sisters of St. Joseph of
    Carondelet
Sisters of St. Joseph of
    Peace
J. Sitnick
J. L. & L. Sitnick
R. Skinner
R. B. Skinner
H. Skott
J. & N. Slais
A. Slater
P. Slater
W. O. Slayman
J. M. Slevin
W. & K. Slick
D. Sloan
R. Sloan
J. & D. Slocum
A. Sloss
E. Sloss
E. Slowikowski
C. & H. Slucki
I. Slutsker
R. Smalley
S. Smallman

C. Smilovitz
B. Smith
B. & C. Smith
D. Smith
E. Anshin Smith
H. E. Smith
M. Smith
M. Smith
M. L. Smith
M. V. Smith
N. Smith
N. Smith
P. N. Smith
R. & J. Smith
R. J. Smith
R. O. Smith
S. Smith
T. Smith
T. I. Smith
T. L. Smith
M. Smolen
J. & T. Smucker
C. L. Snavely
W. Snead
H. Snyder
J. Snyder
B. & B.J. Sobin
P. Sobocinski
S. & S. Socolar
J. Soderberg
D. & M. Sollenberger
M. Solnit
D. Solomon
E. Solomon
E. M. Solomon
G. Solomon
I. & Y. Solomon
J. Solomon
K. Solomon
Mr. & Mrs. S. Solomon
A. & C. Somkin
M. Sopchak
H. Sorkin
Mr. & Mrs. B.J.
  Soukup
D. T. Southall
A. Spanel
R. Spangler
J. Speier, III
L. Speiser
J. Speisman
J. Spencer
J. J. & W. H. Spencer
W. & P. Spicer
J. & A. Spielberg
M. A. Spielberg
R. D. Spiller
D. & K. Spinning-
  Gordon
D. G. Sprague
St. Mark Presbyterian
  Church
A. W. Staats
F.W. & V. Stamler
M. Stanford
M. A. Stang

E. A. Stanley
P. D. L. Stansky
I. Stark
L. & B. Stark
K. Starr
N. Starr
G. Stassen
E. R. Stauffer
M. Stavroulakis
G. & E. Steadman
H. O. Stearns
P. & P. Stearns
D. Stebbins
R. F. Steed
J. & P. Stehle
Dr. & Mrs. E. Stein
B. Stensky
A. Stephens & J.
  Cowles
D. R. Stephens
E. P. Stern
L. S. Stern
A. Sternberg
T. Sterne
J. Stetson
K. Stetson
K. A. Stevens
B. & M. Stevenson
G. & E. Stevenson
T. D. Stevenson
W. T. Linney
J. Stewart
P. O. Stewart
S. Stewart
J. & L. Still
K. Stiven
K. S. Stokes
A.H. & D. Stone
D. Stone
D.A. Stone
J. N. Stone
L. E. Stone
P. Stone
R. & E. Stone
W. A. Stone
R. Stopol
J.A. Stoughton
P. Stoughton
M. Stout
J. Stovicek
A. Stowell
D.C. Strain
J.W. Strange
W. Strathmann
J.S. Strauch
A. & C. Strauss
L. Stretch
O. & J. Strickland
B. Strieb
C. & A. Stroebel
B. Stuart
E. Stults
M. Sturm
E. Sturtevant
P. Suarez
M. & R. Sugarman

D. Sullivan
J. Sullivan
D. Sumin
L. Summer
D.S. Summers
A. & E. Summit
D.M. Sutherland
H. Sutherland
P.D. Sutley
R.F. Sutton
S. Svanoe
J.L. Swanson
S. Swart
E. Sweda Jr.
A. & M. Swedlund
G.L. Sweetnam
S.R. Swift
T. Swift
E. Tambak
B.M. Tanner
D.M. Tarbell
R. Tarbell
M. Tarlow
M.M. Tartell
C. Tatsumi
E. Tattelman
B. & H. Taylor
C.L. Taylor
E. & W. Taylor
I. & R. Taylor
J. Taylor
K. Taylor
D.S. Teague
G.H. Tederick
D.F. Teitelbaum
P.R. Temple
C. Tendler
N. Teply
M. Terefenko
I. Terkel
H. Terrell
E. Tews
E. Thaemert
M. Thayer
M. Themba
V. Thoemmes
K. Tholin
A.P. Thomas
G. Thomas
G.W. & B.P. Thomas
J.R. Thomas
L. Thomas
M.M. Thomas
P. & S. Thomas
V.E. Thomas
A.J. Thompson
C. Thompson
D. Thompson
E.H. Thompson, Jr.
J.M. Thompson
K. Thompson
M.N. Thompson
R. & S. Thompson
W. Thompson
K. Thomsen
E. Thomson

H.C. & D. Thorman
R.F. Thorne
M.G. Thornton
D.J. Tierney
E.H. Tilford
D.R. Titcomb
P. Titcomb
E. Tobach
G. & R. Tobias
J. Todd
P. Todd
A. Todd-Rink
F.A. Toellnew
A. Toft
C. Tolleson
H.E. Tolley
J. Tompkins
F. Topik
J. Tracy
V. Taiman
A. Trattner
H. L. Travis
M. Trelease
R. Trenholm
N. Trent
J. Trider
B. Triggs
N. K. Tripp
O. Trippel
J. C. Trombold
D. Truly
J & S. E. Tucker
N. E. & A. B. Tucker
S. A. Tuller
J. & M. R. Turk
J. P. Turkiewicz
A. Turner & C. Bax
J. &N. Tuthill
M. J. Twohy
L. P. Tyler
R. W. Tyler
F. Tyson
S. Udin
D. Ulmer
W. Umber
S. Umpleby
J. J. Underhill
R. Ungar
B. & C. Unsworth
O. & M. Updike
R.M. Uphaus
F. Utevsky
D. & J. Vacheron
A. Vagnucci
D. & A. Valaskovic
F. Z. Van Dyke
M. C. Van Evera
J. C. Van Itallie
C. Vanacker
B. Vandenhoeck
G. M. Vanderloop
K. Vaneman
S. & D. Vanhoeven
D. Vantomme
P. Varkell
A. Vena

INFACT:
21 YEARS OF EFFECTIVE CAMPAIGNING TO STOP CORPORATE ABUSES

INFACT is a nonpartisan national grassroots organization whose purpose is to stop life-threatening abuses by transnational corporations and increase their accountability to people around the world. Since 1977, INFACT has been educating the public about dangerous abuses of power by giant corporations—and organizing millions of people to take action to change corporate behavior.

The Infant Formula Campaign

On January 26, 1984, representatives from what had started out six and one-half years earlier as a small grassroots campaign met with representatives of Nestlé, the world's largest food company, to end a boycott campaign that had spread to over ten countries. The occasion marked the first time in history that a movement of ordinary people had forced a transnational corporation to deal directly with them at the negotiating table. The many accomplishments of this unprecedented international grassroots consumer campaign include major contributions to the passage of the World Health Organization's International Code of Marketing for Breast Milk Substitutes in 1981, and worldwide exposure of a deadly corporate practice that had been kept hidden. Nestlé came to the negotiating table with INFACT and our allies, and agreed to abide by this Code after intense economic pressure changed the cost-benefit ratio for the corporation to engage in these deadly abuses.

The Nuclear Weaponmakers Campaign

INFACT's next campaign, from 1984-1993, focused public attention on the corporate role in shaping national security policy, and targeted industry leader and trendsetter General Electric for its role in promoting and producing nuclear weapons. Over four million people actively participated in the Campaign by boycotting GE. This boycott helped push industry leader GE out of the nuclear weapons business. INFACT researched and produced the film *Deadly Deception: General Electric, Nuclear Weapons and Our Environment*—winner of the 1991 Academy Award for Best Documentary: Short Subject. By exposing the devastating human and environmental consequences of nuclear weapons production, *Deadly Deception* is an enduring tool to maintain public resolve against another nuclear weapons build-up.

The Tobacco Industry Campaign

Today, INFACT's organizing centers around two major programs. Through the Tobacco Industry Campaign, launched in 1993, consumers and health advocates are challenging Philip Morris and RJR Nabisco to stop addicting new young customers around the world, and to stop manipulating public policy in the interest of tobacco profits. The Tobacco Industry Boycott is a growing liability for Philip Morris's Kraft and RJR's Nabisco food brands, and has fostered shareholder pressure to free these businesses from their deadly association with tobacco. The Human Toll of Tobacco Project, a collection of photos and stories in memory of loved ones lost to tobacco, is a powerful tool for community-based organizing and educational outreach. INFACT's campaign visibility has generated a public outcry to prevent youth-oriented tobacco marketing, creating a climate of support for full Food and Drug Administration (FDA) authority to regulate the tobacco industry.

The Hall of Shame Campaign

With 21 years of experience, INFACT is a key organization challenging "business as usual" in the political arena. The Hall of Shame Campaign began in 1996 by shining a spotlight on corporate influence and access in the US elections. To date, five corporations have been formally inducted through public events: Philip Morris, RJR Nabisco, Dow Chemical, Waste Management, and Columbia/HCA Healthcare. INFACT activist leaders are widely exposing the human toll of corporate power throughout our political system, and confronting Board members and other top decision makers of Hall of Shame corporations with the impact of their abusive practices on public health, the environment, and democracy.

INFACT Campaign Headquarters
256 Hanover Street
Boston, MA 02113
Phone: 617-742-4583
FAX: 617-367-0191
e-mail: infact@igc.apc.org
www.infact.org